SEFER HA-BAHIR

*The Ultimate Guide to Understanding the
Bahir and Its Influence on Kabbalah and
Jewish Mysticism*

Your Free Gift (only available for a limited time)

Thanks for getting this book! If you want to learn more about various spirituality topics, then join Mari Silva's community and get a free guided meditation MP3 for awakening your third eye. This guided meditation mp3 is designed to open and strengthen ones third eye so you can experience a higher state of consciousness. Simply visit the link below the image to get started.

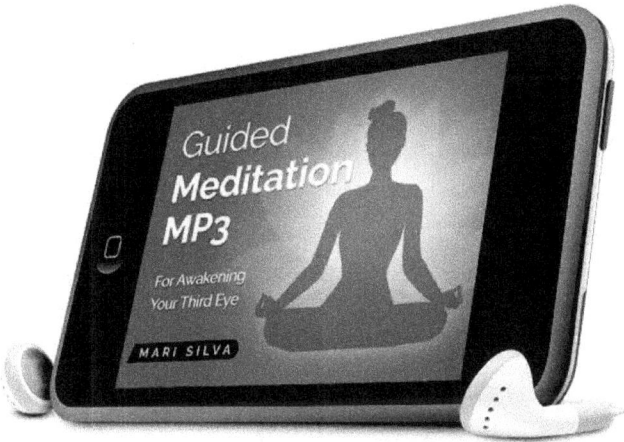

https://spiritualityspot.com/meditation

Contents

Introduction

While minimal in content, the Sefer ha-Bahir is one pillar of Kabbalistic thought.

Through the centuries, scholars have debated authorship; the book is really a collection of writings. Conglomerated, glossed, and redacted, the Sefer ha-Bahir is accredited to multiple authors whose contributions to the book consist of disparate fragments, collected to follow the book's theme – Creation and the role of the Hebrew Alphabet in that Creation. But that's not the only theory at work when you're talking about this ancient – or not so ancient book. Its mysteries have prompted much conflicting scholarship.

Those reading will most likely know Sefer ha-Bahir's most enduring legacy is that of the sefirot. These ten emissaries were first described in this book, and its Kabbalistic colleague, the Sefer Yetzirah. But it's here we find the locus classicus of the Etz Chaim – the Tree of Life – formed of the ten sefirot, each of which represents an attribute of God (a designation which followed the introduction of the sefirot in this book), Sefer ha-Bahir applies a midrashic, mystical interpretation to the Genesis Creation narrative.

Consisting of 140 passages arranged and presented by scholar Gershom Scholem, Sefer ha-Bahir has driven centuries of study and commentary. The book itself is an exegetical roadmap to the Creation narrative found in Genesis, the first of the five books of the Torah.

As you read, I'll share with you the deep mysteries of this book, the sages, scribes, and scholars who form part of its long history and its influence on both Jewish Mysticism and Rabbinical Judaism over many centuries.

To pursue these mysteries is to find the core truths driving Kabbalistic thought and study. At the center of those truths is Creation itself and where humanity stands in the Created Order.

Now, let's journey into one of the Kabbalah's most anciently-rooted and formative texts – the Sefer ha-Bahir – the Book of Brilliance.

A friendly note to readers: All Biblical quotations are taken from the Oxford New Revised Standard Version. Translation of passages from Sefer ha-Bahir is attributable to Aryeh Kaplan's magisterial translation. It's also worth noting that chapter and verse divisions may vary between Hebrew and English in various translations of the Hebrew Scriptures.

Chapter One: Fragments of Brilliance

The truth about the Sefer ha-Bahir is that it's more like an unfinished puzzle than a book. Consisting of fragmentary parables, loosely arranged under themes relating to Creation, the Sefer ha-Bahir is a mystery in many respects, confounding scholars and sages until the present day. First published in 1176 in Provence, France, a medieval center of Kabbalistic thought and study, Sefer ha-Bahir continues to inform Kabbalah as a whole. The literature addressing the contents of Sefer ha-Bahir and the sefirot is voluminous, produced over many centuries.

Sefer ha-Bahir is, in fact, the acknowledged locus classicus or original text of the idea of the sefirot and the Etz Chaim or Tree of Life. But the mystical attributes of what's vaguely described in the book were formed years later. And so, the Sefer ha-Bahir seeded a mystical movement within Judaism that continues to grow in multifarious ways, even in the present day and even outsides the bounds of Judaism itself.

That almost two millennia of influence attributable to such a fractured book, with parables that sometimes end mid-sentence, speaks of Sefer ha-Bahir's enduring power. While physically, the text is rather limited compared to other works in the Kabbalistic canon, religiously, philosophical, and intellectually, it's incredibly rich.

Its position as an ancient text, which serves as a support for an old tradition of mysticism within Judaism, is also deeply important, culturally. In the context of Judaism, the Sefer ha-Bahir has created bridges and incursions in the Jewish religious world, which have transformed the community.

For all these reasons, we'll discuss in this chapter the text's journey toward purported dating and agreed-upon authorship. (My diplomatic way of saying there are differences of opinion.)

Ancient or Not So Ancient

Dating the Sefer ha-Bahir is a topic of dispute, but the majority opinion of secular scholars is that it was produced early in the 13th Century and written by many authors.

But Nachmanides (1194 – 1270 CE) was the first known scholar to name Nehunya ben HaKanah (1st Century, otherwise unknown) as the book's author. Nachmanides also wrote of Sefer ha-Bahir as "the Midrash R. Nehunya ben HaKanaha," referred to in the former's famed Torah commentary in its opening line.

Nachmanides (known by the acronym RAMBan) was a respected scholar in the Middle Ages from the Sephardic or Spanish wing of Judaism, so his opinion has erred on the side of religious scholarship.

For this book, I suggest you take neither of those dates (obviously affecting authorship) as gospel, forming your opinions as we discuss Sefer ha-Bahir further. This suggestion is made in the spirit of the subject, which is part of Kabbalah – a mystical discipline that encourages individual scholarship and exploration, based on the writings of the sages and the Holy books of Judaism. Making up your own mind and choosing your interpretative framework is, no doubt, part of the reason you're here.

The Name

"Now, no one can look on the light when it is bright in the skies when the wind has passed and cleared them."

Job 37:21

The English translation of Sefer ha-Bahir is "The Book of Brilliance." Brilliance may be translated in many ways from the original Hebrew, including "illumination" or simply "light."

In the Job passage, "the light when it is bright in the skies" is the brilliance of God. But the passage tells us that its intensity is unbearable to that point that "no one can look." It speaks of clouds, alluding to a concealed brilliance that may not be looked upon. This is the same veiled God encountered by Moses in the cleft of the rock (Exodus 33:22).

And it's within the ten sefirot that the full brilliance of God, unobscured by clouds, is concealed. The metaphor speaks to an unwritten truth to guide readers to a fuller understanding of that brilliance in the sefirot.

Acting as God's ambassadors to humanity, the sefirot bear within them the whole truth of God's attributes, held within metaphysical worlds that interact to create. The sefirot's emergence in the Sefer ha-Bahir is its dominant theme – a hidden God reaching out to humanity.

And so, Sefer ha-Bahir is named to reflect the brilliance of God, accessibility to God through the intellect, the interpretation of and reflection on the sefirot and their significance, the Hebrew alphabet, and its role in the Created Order.

The Text

It was originally Israeli scholar Gershom Scholem (1997 - 1982) who divided Sefer ha-Bahir into 140 distinct passages as a series of parables/pericopes/portions of text.

Gershom Scholem, originally from Germany, was one of the foremost scholars of Kabbalah but was never a member of the communities which were most pivotal to its development - the Hassidim. Specifically, Scholem was a secularist who emigrated to Israel and pursued his fascination with Kabbalah and its voluminous canon. We'll talk more about him later.

Written in Hebrew and Aramaic, the intention of the work is midrashic. Midrash is an exegetical tradition in Jewish scholarship, using comparative sources to arrive at an interpretation. In this instance, the text being examined is the Genesis Creation narrative.

Sefer ha-Bahir re-visions the Creation narrative, seeing it through mystical eyes. Drilling down through the text to the layers of meaning that lay beneath it, the book redefines the intention of the scripture portions employed, using a distinct lens.

Meaning in the text is attached not only to the phonetic features of the Hebrew letters and the meaning of the words they form, but it's also attached to the shape of the letters and space which accommodates them. It's further attached to vowel pointings and cantillations (which indicate emphasis for sung prayer).

Structure

Gershom Scholem's 140 passages are parables that serve as commentaries, addressing specific portions of the Creation narrative in Genesis.

Consisting of five distinct sections, the parables in each section don't always address the topic at hand but rather roughly adhere to a theme. These are:

One	Creation narrative commentary
Two	The Hebrew alphabet cast as Creation's substance
Three	The sefirot and the seven voices
Four	Etz Chaim (the model of the ten sefirot)
Five	The soul's mysteries; summation

One of the primary differences between Sefer ha Bahir and Sefer Yetzirah, thematically, is found in both of the sefirot descriptions. Sefer Yetzirah is primarily focused on the sefirot in numerical terms. Sefer ha-Bahir is more focused on their role in Creation as God's attributes and their operation in concert with the Hebrew alphabet. The two books merely apply different criteria in their interpretation, with the same goal – revealing God's brilliance through the sefirot, bearing within them God's attributes. The concealed brilliance of God is accessible through the sefirot to the student who apprehends their mysteries.

In the next section, we'll explore the complex history of the book.

Folklore and Critical Study

Whether we choose to accept it or not, folklore almost always develops from a grain of historical truth. Folklore may either further illuminate certain realities or obscure them by distorting the facts.

With Sefer ha-Bahir, there may be more to the folkloric assertions about the book than there appears to be when held up against secular/critical scholarship.

Kabbalists – those who study and apply Kabbalistic principles - are most likely to cleave to the argument in favor of 1st Century authorship (R. Nehunya). The Medieval Kabbalists, like Nachmanides, as discussed above, were clear that the book was received by them as disparate pieces of a whole. These were said to have been discovered, piece by piece. As we've read, this claim is well-supported by the fragmentary nature of the text.

Critical, secular study of the Sefer ha-Bahir has concluded that the book was written in the 13th Century, attributing it to Isaac the Blind (circa 1160 – 1235) or possibly to students of his, among other scribes.

Modern scholarship rejects this claim, acknowledging an older origin for the book, with its genesis in Sefer Raza Rabba.

No longer extant in its entirety, Ronit Meroz has dated at parts of Sefer ha-Bahir to 10th Century Babylon. Applying a critical linguistic approach, Meroz has stated that the use of Babylonian pointing indicates vowels used during that time, which later became extinct, is found in the Sefer ha-Bahir. She recognized that other parts of the book reflected language usage in Provence, France, during the 12th Century.

Ronit Meroz, Professor of Jewish Philosophy and Talmud at the University of Jerusalem, is joined by scholars Gershom Scholem and Moshe Idel in her hypothesis of the ancient origins of Sefer ha-Bahir. These two scholars also conclude this based on the similarities between the book's contents and writings emanating from the First Century's Jewish Gnosticism. I will talk about that a little later.

For now, it's important to note that what is indicated by the scholarship is that both folklore and critical secular scholarship are somewhat vindicated. While there is no definitive answer, it's clear that the ancient influence of earlier works expressing Jewish Mysticism's early manifestations is present in Sefer ha-Bahir. But in the tradition of Holy Writings, there are often multiple contributors over long periods.

The Great Secret

Sefer Raza Rabba - Book of the Great Secret - no longer exists. Still, the book is mentioned throughout the 9th, 10th, and 11th centuries by Babylonian sages and in the works of Daniel al-Qumisi (died 946), the Karaite sage of Jerusalem.

In the tradition of Merkavah Mysticism (100 BCE - 1000 CE), the book expounds on the Merkavah (Chariot) described in the Book of Ezekiel and contains a great deal of magical content. The book also includes the naming of demons, angels, and gematria (assigning numerical values to letters to gain deeper meanings in the text).

Considered a midrashic work in the Merkavah tradition, the book is mentioned in a commentary by Moshe ha-Darshan, a 13th Century sage of Narbonne, calling the book "Ha Sod ha Gadol" - the Great Secret.

As I've said earlier, Raza Rabba no longer exists in its original form or forms. It's believed that there was more than one version of the book in circulation at one time. But it lives on in its intimate link to the later Sefer ha-Bahir.

Themes and ideas in the Raza Rabba were further developed in Sefer ha-Bahir, including the ten sefirot. While appearing in Raza Rabba, the sefirot only remains a fragment of what was written by whoever was responsible for compiling the book. There is no indication of any development of the sefirot's symbolic significance, but the link between them is there. Raza Rabba became a literary resource for critical editing to Sefer ha-Bahir, over time, drawing on its serial appearances in the writings of the Babylonian sages and ha-Darshan.

Key Scholarship

Sefer ha-Bahir is best described as a collection of miniature sermons, delivered by sages familiar to readers with a few apocryphal figures thrown in by contributors.

The passages, as arranged by Gershom Scholem, consist of a variety of layers of contributions added through the ages. Scholem argued for the text's Gnostic origin, with the earliest portions of the text written in the Ancient Near East or derived from Ancient Near Eastern writings.

Scholem further pointed to contributions emanating from Germany and suggested that the latest additions came from the late 12th Century. Specifically, he attributed these to writers in Languedoc, in the south of France.

Scholem's hypothesis on authorship and dating for Sefer ha-Bahir is increasingly accepted as accurate by contemporary scholars. However, Moshe Idel contends that Scholem's appeal to the text's Gnostic origin was more likely to derive from later channels of thought in Judaism. Also, Scholem's assertion that part of the book originated in Germany is gaining scholarly influence.

Haviva Pedaya, of Ben-Gurion University in Jerusalem, has also explored the interplay between Hellenistic and Jewish thought as a subtext in Sefer ha-Bahir, pointing to the melting pot of philosophies in the Ancient Near East, which likely influenced the book's authors through time. The continuing influence of Hellenism through the Middle Ages highlights the necessity to consider Sefer ha-Bahir as, at least partially, a product of the confluence of mysticism and philosophy.

Using the words "tohu" and "bohu" in the text (found in Genesis 1:2, meaning "formless" and "void") is a clue to the question of Hellenistic influence, specifically, that of Neo-Platonist thought in the question of matter and how it was manipulated at Creation. We'll talk about this feature of Bahir near the end of this book.

As you can see from this chapter's information, what we know as *Sefer ha-Bahir* is not really a book. Many speculate that the "book" was thrown to the wind and then given to the sages, who re-assembled it – in the wrong order.

But what matters about the Sefir ha-Bahir is its position as the first exposition on the "10 utterances" – the sefirot themselves, characterized as linguistic realities. The latter part of the book is where these are discussed at length.

The King

A feature of the Sefer ha-Bahir, which is of interest, is using an analogy to underline the lesson being taught. To make its parables coherent, analogous figures like the King, his daughter, and servants of the Royal Household and places like the palace gardens are used.

These analogous representations are used as expository devices for the Hebrew Scripture portion that accompanies each parable and then the parable itself. The King and his household are used by the author(s) of Sefer ha-Bahir to illuminate a central truth in the related text, which forms the paragraph/parable.

These analogous figures are often used playfully, but their purpose is to illuminate this scribe's intention by creating a visual that penetrates the meaning of what's being presented.

To illustrate the purpose of the analogous figures, let's look at Paragraph 16 in Section I of the Sefer ha-Bahir. (NB: Rabbi Rahumai has been placed in quotations, as he is unknown beyond this work and in the Zohar. While he may have existed, it's not known whether this parable is attributable to him or not. Some rabbinical personalities in Sefer ha-Bahir are fictitious; others, like its pseudepigraphic author, Nehunya ben HaKanah, were known and acknowledged sages).

In this paragraph, "Rabbi Rahumai" states that light existed before Creation, providing a pretext in Psalm 97:2, namely, "Cloud and gloom surround Him," linking it to Genesis 1:3, "And God said, 'let there be light' and there was light."

"Rabbi Rahumai" then employs the persona of the King who yearned intensely for a son. The King, seeing a beautiful crown, buys it for the yet-to-be-born son. When he's asked how he knows that his yet unconceived son will be worthy of it, the King says, "Be still. This is what arises in thought."

The figure of the King is used as an example of God's longing for Creation, so strong that the inspiration of light arrives before Creation, just as the crown for the King's longed-for son expresses his yearning. His exhortation to those who question the purchase of the Crown for a yet-unborn son who may prove unworthy is to "be still." The King's thought is presented as an inspiration, just as God's thought at Creation was driven by the same.

By employing Hebrew Scripture and calling on characters like the King, the author tells a story that illuminates a much larger truth about God's longing for Creation.

Our next chapter will discuss the sefirot, what they are and who this mysterious Adam Kadmon fellow might be.

Chapter Two: Ten Utterances That Created the World

In Sefer ha-Bahir, we first encounter the sefirot being described as emanations of God, but in a very different way than they are described in the Sefer Yetzirah. Unlike the Sefer Yetzirah, there is no numeric value assigned to them. Rather, each sefirah corresponds to a stage in the Biblical Creation narrative and an associated Biblical character. That does not imply the presence of gematria in the text of Bahir, but that presence is not nearly as potent as it is in Yetzirah.

The ten utterances represent instances in the Genesis narrative of Creation featuring the phrase "And God said." All 10 of these occur in the first chapter of the Book, between verses 3 and 30 (Genesis 1:3, 1:6, 1:9, 1:11, 1:14-15, 1:20, 1:26, 1:28, 1:29-30).

Just as there are ten fingers on human hands and ten toes on human feet, there are ten utterances that wrought Creation from the depths of the Creator's Divine Will. And just as there are ten utterances, there are ten sefirot emanating from the same source. In every stage and every creative utterance, there are the sefirot, revealing to us the essential nature of God.

It's in Sefer ha-Bahir that we also find the first representation of the sefirot as Etz Chaim. The Tree of Life serves as a visual organization of God's attributes, positioning each attribute in the tree, where they're arranged to the right, left, and down the center of this graphic device.

But the Tree of Life has a second identity – that of Adam Kadmon or Primordial Man. This is not the Adam in the Bible. Adam Kadmon serves as a human-shaped representation of creaturely humanity, embodying its most ideal representation and God's unsullied intention for the Created Order.

Also found in Sefer ha-Bahir is the nascent idea of tzimtzum (contraction), which first appeared in the Kabbalistic tradition in the Tikkunei ha-Zohar or Rectifications (also translated as "repairs") of the Zohar (1558). It contains a formula for repairing a broken Creation, in which God is concealed from what has been created. We'll talk more about that shortly but, for the purposes of this chapter, let's examine the ten sefirot from the standpoint of Kabbalah as a whole.

Meet the Sefirot

The sefirot are not only God's ambassadors. "Ambassadors" is something of a shallow description, in truth.

The sefirot might be described as conduits through which the Divine energy flows, but even that would fail to convey the mystery of what the sefirot are. Before we meet them in person, it's necessary to understand the intention of the sefirot and the purpose they serve in Kabbalah.

Each of the ten sefirot interacting within the framework of Etz Chaim encompasses a Divine attribute. So, perhaps the most convenient way to describe the sefirot is "emanations." Arranged in the Tree of Life in columns with three on the left, three on the right, and three down the center, the sefirot are conjoined and interdependent and interactive, while separately encompassing an essential trait of God.

As the tree of life stood in the middle of the Creation narrative's Garden of Eden (Genesis 2:9), so the Tree of Life stands in the middle of Kabbalah and its spiritual methodology for approaching God. According to the truths revealed in the sefirot and their creative interaction, Etz Chaim is the way to God. But that's not the whole truth.

The eternal Tree is God, undivided and singular, presented in a format that explains the reality we stand before, in our unknowing state. The sefirot are the fruit of the Holy One, available only to those willing to go out on a limb to (reverently) partake.

Let's meet the sefirot, starting on the left side of the tree. You'll note a corresponding part of the human body listed next to the English translation for each sefirot's Hebrew name.

Binah - Understanding - left brain

Gevurah - Might - left arm, hands, fingers

Hod - Splendor - left leg, foot, toes

On the central axis of the tree, we find:

Keter - Crown - skull

Tiferet - Beauty - torso

Yesod - Foundation - sex organ

Malchut/Shekhinah - Kingdom/Divine Presence - mouth

Finally, on the right side, from the top:

Chochmah - Wisdom - right brain

Chesed - Lovingkindness - right arm, hands, fingers

Netzach - Victory - right leg, foot, toes

The arrangement of these Divine emanations, personified by the sefirot, follow three axes running parallel to each other, vertically. In Hebrew, these are called kavim. Each axis represents a sphere or characterization of Divine activity.

Running between the sefirot's three axes is tzinorot. These are the actual conduits of the interaction between the ten emanations. These conduits run the creative power of the Divine, enabling energy beyond human understanding to operate and express itself.

The sefirot, which connects directly to their tzinorot, suggest common types of activities between implicated contact points, creating a dynamic, energetic Tree unlimited in its power and potential to reveal the Divine.

But as we've touched on earlier, Etz Chaim also represents the form of Adam Kadmon – Primordial Man. And so, the Tree of Life is re-visioned in Sefer ha-Bahir and its cousin text, the Sefer Yetzirah, as a living expression of God's attributes. Thus, the sefirot are part of a construct that reveals God to humanity and resurrects God's intentions in creating humanity – like a giant so close to God as to be distinguished from Creation itself. In the section below about Adam Kadmon, we'll explore Primordial Man's anthropomorphized concept and its place in Kabbalah.

The intention of the Sefer ha-Bahir's representation of the sefirot is to associate them with the stages of the Divine's efforts in Creation. Because Creation exists as a direct expression of God's internal landscape, it's only the culmination of that process revealed in the physical world we perceive. Before the Creation of this world, the final stage of the process, there were others, all both transcending and inherent to the final product.

The sefirot are a living organism, described variously but immutability dynamic. A sole organism rife with spiritual meaning and Divine reason, the sefirot permeate reality at every level.

More than just emissaries, the sefirot are the cloudless day on which it becomes uniquely possible to recognize God's attributes alive in the Creation our human bodies are part of. Etz Chaim is more than a graphic representation. It's a detailed model of God's intimate relationship with the Created Order and humanity's role in that relationship.

Adam Kadmon

Primordial Man is a central theme in understanding Kabbalistic thought, especially about the sefirot and their centrality as a nexus of God's interaction with humanity.

Adam Kadmon stands as an icon of the Adam of the Garden – both not the Adam of the Garden and a semiotic representation of him, simultaneously. This tension between "is" or "is not" is familiar when discussing Kabbalah. But the same is true of most theology, in which the idea of tension is a recurring theme. For example, the fact that God is both transcendent and immanent is similarly counter-intuitive but integral to the whole in Judaism, Christianity, and Islam.

Adam Kadmon is more than just an icon. The figure of a man, when seen in the model of Etz Chaim, corresponds, in its constituent parts, to the sefirot, as noted above. Again, humanity is centered, but with the attributes of God imposed upon its creaturely body, via the metaphysical proxy of Adam Kadmon.

One of Sefer ha-Bahir's most compelling themes is that of Creation and the role of language, vowel pointings, and cantillations in that Creation. In the same tradition of linguistic mysticism as Sefer Yetzirah, the book chooses the Hebrew language as an active agent in Creation, standing as the eternal, creative Word of God. We'll be discussing this theme later in this volume.

The Kabbalistic model of Creation has become, through the magisterial writing of Isaac Luria (1534 – 1572 CE), a complex and systematic undertaking, seeking to apprehend the motivations of a God most consider inscrutable. Part of Luria's model of Creation was a spiritual cataclysm, occasioned by what we can only assume is one of God's greatest disappointments – the Adam of the Garden.

And so, Adam Kadmon is an icon of Adam, an errant child of the garden, metaphysically existing as a higher version of himself in a realm near the concealed God far from the Garden defiled by his decision to take a bite of that notorious apple.

In the Beginning

"Rabbi Nehunyah ben HaKanah said: One verse (Job 37:21) states, "And now they do not see the light, it is brilliant (Bahir) in the skies... [round about God in terrible majesty]."

Another verse, however, (Psalm 18:12), states, "He made darkness His hiding place." It is also written (Psalm 97:2), "Cloud and gloom surround Him." This is an apparent contradiction.

A third verse comes and reconciles the two. It is written (Psalm 139:12), "Even darkness is not dark to You. The night shines like daylight and darkness are the same."

The passage above is the first in Sefer ha-Bahir's treatment of the Genesis Creation narrative, and to move on to our next chapter, which will describe the role of Primordial Man in the Kabbalistic model of Creation following Luria, we need to examine what's being said here.

While the passage is notable, being framed as a saying from the pseudepigraphic First Century author of the book, Nehunya ben HaKanah, what's most interesting about it is the seeds of later interpretation by Isaac Luria and his student Chaim Vital (1542 – 1620 CE), among others.

Beginning with a (previously quoted) passage from the Book of Job, which roots Sefer ha-Bahir's name in the Bible, the passage moves on to the concealment of God (tzimtzum, which we'll discuss shortly) and finally, a reconciliation of the two apparently competing visions of the Divine expressed in the two preceding verses, in which "darkness and light are the same" to God.

Again, the theme of tension arises with God defined as both too brilliant and glorious to behold but simultaneously concealed in darkness, far from any scrutiny. And the passage, whomever it's attributable to, is the basis for later Kabbalistic thought regarding the concealment of God in the process of Creation. The Divine is both shown forth in brilliance and concealed in darkness.

And in this, we can begin to see what service the sefirot, united in Etz Chaim/Adam Kadmon, perform for the Divine. Acting as the light of God, God may maintain both contact and concealment in Holy "isolation."

As we can see in the Psalm 18 quote, the concealment of God is in the Bible, then brought into Sefer ha-Bahir. As we move into reading about the Kabbalistic explanation of Creation and how it all came to be, it's useful to note the seeds of the idea of tzimtzum planted in the Bible itself.

But how did God come to be concealed? Why did God "contract" into metaphysical "isolation"?

This question is key to understanding the sefirot and their intimacy with the Creator.

So, let's start at the beginning - the very beginning - of the Genesis Creation narrative.

"In the beginning, when God created the heavens and the earth, the earth was a formless void and darkness covered the face of the deep, while a wind from God swept over the face of the waters."

Genesis 1: 1 - 2

Genesis presents God as a wind, sweeping over the watery darkness of Creation's potential - a "formless void."

In the original Hebrew of the passage, the words for "formless void" are "tohu wa bohu." The phrase is also found in Isaiah 34:11, translating as "Primordial chaos." The word "tohu" is found throughout the Book of Isaiah, usually meaning "vanity." "Bohu," however, is only seen in 3 places in the Hebrew Scriptures. The third instance is seen in Jeremiah 4:23, translating as "waste and void."

The phrase, when examined, hints at materiality, which presents itself as potential. It is not yet "something." It is "something-in-waiting."

Tohu wa bohu is the raw, lifeless material that awaits the enlivening hand of the Creator. Sefer ha-Bahir dwells on both that formless void and its role in the process of Creation.

5th Century BCE Greek philosopher, Parmenides, stated "ex nihilo nihil fit" – "from nothing, nothing comes." If the vision of Genesis is correct, then so was the Ancient Greek. Because Primordial Chaos was not "nothing." Rather, it was matter awaiting an organizing force to make sense of it.

What's striking about the opening scene in the Drama of Creation described in Genesis is the absence of myth. There is no elaboration on why God is moving over the waters or why the "wind from God" would move over the waters of Chaos to enliven them. This speaks to the unlimited agency of an unknowable Creator, making the passage unusual in its Ancient Near Eastern setting, which was teeming with such narratives of how the universe came to be.

Enuma Elish (1750 BCE, Sumeria) and other regional Creation narratives involve an element of the fantastical. For example, Enuma Elish describes the elevation of the god, Marduk, to the leadership of the Sumerian Pantheon. In the Genesis Creation story, there is only the wind of God and Primordial Chaos. No motivation is stated. There are no other Gods. There is just the One God and the raw stuff that will, by God's hand, become the Created Order.

Not by cleaving the evil Tiamat in two does the God of Genesis create rivers and mountains. The God of Genesis merely speaks Creation into being by way of the ten utterances.

There is a matter-of-fact quality to the story of Creation in Genesis. While quietly dramatic, there is no cleaving of a Primordial Snake Goddess or drama in which one god arises to reign over a teeming pantheon of others. It's merely a quiet story of wind and water, darkness and formless chaos, waiting to be born as "something."

And in this quiet tale, God's words and breath figure as the creative agents. Breath forces the words from the mouth of the Holy One, bringing into being all that is, formed by a will that gives life through the spoken word.

And in the Kabbalah's elaboration on the simplicity of Genesis's description of Creation, we see one of the primary concerns of Sefer ha-Bahir – the primacy of the Hebrew language as the instigating force active in God's magnum opus.

But before we can talk about the Hebrew language's creative power, we need to take a walk through the Kabbalah's complex elaboration on the Creation narrative. In it, God is hidden away in the darkness to make space for has "arisen in thought" and then been wrought.

At the center of Creation's treatment by Kabbalah is the figure of Adam Kadmon. More than just a model of Primordial Man, Adam Kadmon is a world unto himself. But why are there two Adams?

What happened that created the need for an anthropomorphized icon, standing as a world unto itself?

To answer that question, we return to the Garden of Eden and the man placed in that Garden. We all know what Adam did to be cast out.

But do we know that Adam, created from the stuff of the earth, dropped the ball? Let's find out about the real sin of Adam and discover how it led to a battle, through time, for the errant soul of humanity.

Chapter Three: A Monkey Wrench in the Works of God

"So God created humankind in his image, in the image of God he created them, male and female he created them."

Genesis 1:27

Being created "in the image of God" - B'tzelem Elohim - is no laughing matter. But in the verse above, in which God does precisely that, we're not talking about the way things look.

We're talking about an ontological reality. The ontology describes the essential nature of things and their place in reality - including the essential nature of the human-animal and its place in Creation.

The creation of humanity in the image of God implies stewardship as stated in Genesis 1:26, in which God gives humanity "dominion" over everything from birds to livestock to "creeping things."

In Christianity, the word "dominion" has been interpreted to align with unlimited power due to the translation of verse 28's instruction to humanity to "...fill the earth and subdue it". But what does "dominion" mean when one has been created in the image of God?

Psalm 8:6 relates, "You have given them dominion over the works of your hands; you have put all things under their feet."

Humanity being placed in such a position due to having been made in the image of God almost sounds as though the human-animal has been created to stand in place of God, but this is a presumptuous interpretation of Primordial Man's role in the Created Order.

Rather, as the image of God in Creation, humanity's role is one of stewardship. Just as a Border Collie herds the sheep on behalf of the farmer, humanity herds the vast Creation's denizens on behalf of God. This is the ontological work of humanity, just as sheep are the ontological work of the Border collie.

For God to tell Primordial Humanity it has been made in the image of God – a God we can't see to check for a resemblance to us - speaks to the arrangement as a partnership. God has no hands. Humans have those. And if humans are made in an inscrutable, ineffable image, then "the image of God" is found in the Divine attributes, which the Created Order not only reflects but contains, in every conceivable detail and fiber.

But the problem with humanity being made in the image of God is that the trust inherent in having taken a decision to do so seems to have been misplaced.

"So when the woman saw that the tree was good for food, and that it was a delight to the eyes, and that the tree was to be desired to make one wise, she took of its fruit and ate; and she also gave some to her husband, who was with her, and he ate."

Genesis 3:6

And he ate.

Adam ate of the Tree of the Knowledge of Good and Evil, so falling from grace in the eyes of God.

But is that the true cataclysm in this narrative? Is the fact that Adam ate the fruit of the tree the true cause of the chasm between God and humanity?

Not according to the Kabbalah's treatment of the Creation narrative.

Ideal Adam

Isaac Luria is easily the most influential of all the Kabbalistic sages, also recognized by the name "Ha'ARI HaKadosh (the Holy Lion) or simply, ARI, as well as ARIzel.

Father of Kabbalah as we know it today, ARI wrote little, but his teachings were widely disseminated via the passion and devotion of his students. From Safed, his influence continued to spread until Luria's interpretation of Creation became synonymous with that accepted by Kabbalists everywhere.

And it's this one which interests us. Because in Luria's vision of Creation, Adam of the Garden is made whole in the spiritualized Adam Kadmon – an ideal version of the creaturely "problem child," Adam.

Elevated from his failed status in Creation, Adam is restored to the idealized state in which the Divine was inspired to create him, becoming the Kabbalistic figure, Adam Kadmon. Just as God's ten utterances resulted in Creation, God's inspiration sparked the Creation of a partner to tend it.

But there was more to Adam's mission on earth than watering plants and feeding animals. His mission was *tikkun* – repair. And what was he to repair?

Adam was to repair the shattered pieces of clay vessels, scattered abroad on the Divine's perfect Creation – the kelipot. Exploding in the darkness of the cosmos, the shattering of these vessels released into Creation all that was to have been contained within them.

Before Adam reached out for that apple he'd been expressly warned not to eat, he'd been given all he required to pick up the pieces of those shattered, scattered vessels. He'd been part of a Divine plan to repair the damage. Having been made in God's image – the Divine template of Adam Kadmon transposed to the Created Order – he'd been put in place as God's hands.

And in that Creation, tikkun had already been accomplished. For God, that seems to have been the whole point, according to Kabbalah.

So, when Adam bit into that juicy, forbidden apple, he created a catastrophe in Creation. The Covenant with the Creator was ruptured. What had been so recently healed was, in a single bite, again wounded. With that single action, Adam undid the tikkun for which his very existence had been pre-destined.

The clue to the importance of humanity in the great scheme of Creation is in its being fashioned "in the image of God." But Kabbalah tells us that the image's impression of the human-animal is much more profound. What's been impressed upon us, through the ideal Adam, are the very attributes of our Creator. In Adam Kadmon, our sublime exemplar, the Light of the Limitless is contained and mediated.

There is a consubstantiality in the relationship between Adam and the Divine, which transcends parental analogies. Adam's Creation is intentional, with a specific purpose in mind for the creature, formed as a realized inspiration of God's plan for Creation. Bearing the image of God is not about body parts. Rather, bearing the image of God is about intention and fidelity to the plan.

Like the King with his crown for an unborn son, God believed in his inspiration.

And this explains why Adam Kadmon's body is Etz Chaim. The Tree of Life provides not just food but the full realization of God's intention – that Creation should be nourished by an agent of the Divine just as the Tree nourishes that agent.

Etz Chaim, being the graphic depiction of the sefirot, is also the graphic depiction of Adam Kadmon – his body. That body consists of the attributes of God contained in the sefirot and continually interacting to show the glory of the Divine in Creation, following the intention of the Creator.

As Adam Kadmon's body is the metaphysical bearer of the sefirot, he's transcended by their agency. And by the agency of the sefirot, humanity is given access to an image of both the Divine and an idealized version of themselves in this, the most complex and transcendent of all God's inspirations.

A Being of Light

Adam Kadmon, while an anthropomorphized figure (said by some to also embody Torah), is not analogous to the Adam of the Garden. Rather, Adam Kadmon is the Divine's inspired notion of a partner – a reflection of God's glory – that acts on earth to realize Creation's plan. Integral to the figure of Adam Kadmon is the fullness of God's Divine breath imparted at Creation and all it contained.

In Etz Chaim, Adam Kadmon is borne into Creation surreptitiously – in disguise. The ten sefirot, their activity is expressing the attributes and intentions of God as impressed upon incarnated Adam, render both the Creator and the Created visible in their most compelling manifestations.

With the failure of humanity to follow through, Adam Kadmon remains in place. There is no concurrent dissipation of the dream of an ideal Adam. The physical teeth of God's partner in the project of tikkun sinking into the apple bear no relation to his idealized metaphysical prototype. That dream lives and not only in God's image but as an entire world unto itself.

Constructed of light and conducting light to lower realms, concluding in the Created Order, Adam Kadmon's position is near the Divine itself, just as the inspiration is from the very mind and heart of the Creator. Denied his creaturely partner, God's prototype of that dream remains ever near, working with the imagination that created it, bearing and diffusing the Divine Light at the Creator's will.

As metaphysical reality and a world unto himself, Adam Kadmon sits nearest the Limitless, serving as a conduit of the Divine Brilliance and as its home. There is a profound longing in the figure of this ideal Adam, embodying the dreams of God for Creation and humanity as a steward.

Adam Kadmon's figure stands as the fullness of the human soul's potential and its purest form as the "image of God." Inextricably linked to its Source, Adam Kadmon also bears within its metaphysical reality – the essence of humanity's collective soul. This is the ideal of the purified soul, perfected and operating in unimpeded unity with the will of the Creator.

Yeshida is also aspirational. In Adam Kadmon, the ideal man and God's intention for humanity, yeshida is the state of the human soul usually ascribed to martyrs and those who sacrifice themselves for the sake of others. And this is the state of Adam Kadmon, the human soul's metaphysical prototype. This is the figure of the human being fully realized.

This is the human that God created and put in the Garden. And while Eve is forever tarnished for plucking and then passing the forbidden fruit to Adam, urging him to eat of it, she is forever exonerated by the fact that God's Covenant was made with Adam. Getting evicted from the Garden seems rather a mild punishment when you think about the chain reaction of dodging his intended purpose and mission - embodying and accomplishing tikkun.

Adam was the monkey wrench in the works of God's intentions for the Created Order. And all it takes is one monkey wrench in the works to bring everything to a grinding halt.

613 Mitzvot

The 613 mitzvot, mystically remembered as having been transmitted to Moses at Mt. Sinai, stand as a spiritual means for pursuing the work of tikkun. While modernism applies to the idea of tikkun in Judaism and in those Christian and Muslim circles in which it's discussed, this is not the intent of tikkun. In the modernist expression of what is essentially a mystical concept, relating directly to Creation, acts directed toward solving a public challenge (poverty, homelessness, violence) are deemed tikkun.

But such acts relate to the material world and conditions prevailing. In the Kabbalistic model, Tikkun refers to spiritual matters and the mystical project of repairing the relationship between God and humanity, thus healing the Created Order.

In this model, the 613 mitzvot -commandments – and their satisfaction by believers - are the heart and soul of tikkun olam (healing the world/Creation).

These laws prescribe both "dos" and "don'ts." In the "don't" column are found 365 mitzvot, corresponding to the number of days in the year. In the "do" column are found 248 mitzvot. These correspond to the number of organs and bones in the human body.

So, the "dos" - the positive actions prescribed by the Law of Moses – are equal to the number of internal organs and bones that comprise the human body. This implies the value of the Divinely created human body and its holiness. In the Kabbalistic model, the light in the metaphysical body of Adam Kadmon has a parallel in the carnal spirituality of the positive mitzvot, numbered to speak of created humanity's sanctified status in the Created Order.

You may be wondering if the 10 Commandments of the Bible form a part of the 613 mitzvot comprising the Law of Moses. The answer to that question is "only two."

These are the first two Commandments, heard issuing from the mouth of God by Moses, and so they are included. The same mouth which had by ten utterances, "spoken" Creation into being, relayed these two Commandments to the Prophet at Sinai. These are the two Commandments relating directly to God's relationship with the Exiled Israelites – that they should "have no other gods before me" (Exodus 20:3) and that they should not "make...an idol" (Exodus 20:4a). The other 611 mitzvot are contained in the Books of Torah.

The practices of "Orthodox" or "right thinking" Jews are defined by the satisfaction of the 613 mitzvot. The rationale is not carceral or punitive. The rationale for centering the mitzvot is tikkun. Further, living by these commandments creates a constant awareness in communities who chose to do so of the presence, omnipotence, and omniscience of God.

Secular observers may deem these practices arcane and rigid, but by recognizing their role in terms of tikkun, the wisdom of these practices within their religious context is discernible.

Ohr Ein Sof

Ohr Ein Sof is the Light of the Divine. This is the light spoken of in the first chapter, where we discovered Sefer ha-Bahir's name in Job 37:21.

This is the Light "no one can look on," without the mediating veil of cloud cover. Speaking to the splendor of the Divine and the inaccessibility of direct contact, the verse explains to us why the Light of the Divine may be experienced only under that veil of cloud cover or perhaps in the cleft of a rock, as Moses once did. Too blindingly brilliant for human eyes, we need a pinhole camera to observe the ultimate illumination.

And it's that brilliance the Sefer ha-Bahir seeks to point the way to, in its fractured way. Through the efforts of Isaac Luria and his student, Chaim Vital, we understand the Ohr Ein Sof as an unbearable radiance that the naked eye can't view.

Chaim Vital, in his text, Etz Chaim (1573), explains the diffusion of the Ohr Ein Sof into Creation as a type of transformation to "created light." While it's not explained whether this transformation is material or merely a trick with mirrors, Vital posited that we could know the light of God only through the veil of matter.

Transformed to creaturely light, the Light of the Divine moves among us, disguised as God's own intentionally uttered creation, in order not to blind us with its brilliance. By appearing incognito in the Created Order and as a created phenomenon, Ohr Ein Sof reduces itself to the status of what its source has created. No longer emanating from the Divine itself, we're able to view it as it hides in plain sight.

We've already touched on tzimtzum, the concealment of God, reading about how the theme arises in Sefer ha-Bahir. Next, we'll read about how the God of glory stoops to conquer by hiding in the darkness, leaving the sefirot to speak eternal truths to Creation.

Chapter Four: Greta Garbo and an Experiment Gone Wrong

"What is the meaning of 'from eternity (me-Olam)?" This means that it must be concealed (he-elam) from the world.

Sefer ha-Bahir, Section I, 10b

Eternity, as I'm sure we can all agree, is a long time. But how long is "long" and what is time, especially when we're discussing something which can't be measured – not unlike the Divine; the Limitless?

The word "eternity" ascribes an arbitrary nature to time. The word also implies that time is stripped of its meaning, having been subsumed under a greater one.

From the Latin "aeternitatum," the original meaning of "eternity" was "enduring" or "permanent." Eternity was described by Aristotle (384 – 322 BCE) as an "unmoved mover." And in the Sefer ha-Bahir and the Kabbalistic model of Creation, it stands as the foundation to, that mover is hidden from view.

Like the Wizard of Oz, God is concealed. But as stated in the verse portion of Sefer ha-Bahir shown above, God is eternity itself – an eternity which "must be concealed from the world."

So concealed, the Divine, having contracted into a space beyond Creation, sends out the Light of the Limitless, disguised as creaturely light. This action limits both the Source of the Light and the Light itself, but that's far from the end of the story of tzimtzum.

As we've read in the previous chapter, Ohr Ein Sof becomes a creature of the Divine from which it emanates, to conceal the full glory of God that "no one can look on." Similarly, the Divine Source of that light, Ein Sof (the Limitless), contracts, becoming "less than" to make space for the Creation that inspiration has provoked.

References to the word "tzimtzum" do not exist in the text. Rather, these were developed later, primarily in the mind of Isaac Luria, who teased out the themes from foundational Kabbalistic texts like Sefer ha-Bahir and Sefer Yetzirah and the Tikkunei ha-Zohar to arrive at a mystical interpretation of the Genesis Creation narrative.

As we've seen in the portions of Sefer ha-Bahir that we've examined so far, the author(s) of the book employed the midrashic technique of comparative interpretation (exegesis) to illuminate the Genesis Creation tale, drawing on the fullness of the Hebrew Scriptures from the Prophets to the Proverbs and Psalms. This work was continued and elaborated on through time until it grew up to become the full flowering of Kabbalistic, mystical interpretation.

We see in the verse featured at the head of this chapter concealment and how eternity (in truth, God) must be hidden, even though the fully-realized concept of tzimtzum was yet to come, with the nascent tzimtzum motifs of Sefer ha-Bahir teeming with questions.

Emanating in Concealment

Isaac Luria's revolutionary treatment of the Sefer ha-Bahir, Sefer Yetzirah, and the Zohar integrated these texts' contents to create a coherent treatment of the Genesis Creation narrative, which mentioned several questions left unanswered in the original text. This became the backbone of Kabbalistic thought, primarily embodied in 4 key concepts:

> **Tzimtzum** - The concealment/contraction of God
>
> **Shevirat ha Kelim** - The shattering of the vessels
>
> **Tikkun** - The repair of Creation through the repair of the Divine/Human partnership
>
> **Parzufim** - The realignment of the sefirot toward the repair of Creation

Of these four concepts or themes, we'll treat the first three in this book to avoid any confusion about the mission we're on, which is to more fully appreciate Sefer ha-Bahir and its place in the canon of Kabbalah.

A discussion of the parzufim is more properly cited in a book about the Zohar, as that's where this 4th concept originates, later developed by Luria as part of his Kabbalistic construct of Creation.

Tzimtzum

According to Luria, it's in tzimtzum, a sudden action based on an instinct of God - that tension between omnipotence and humility is seen. God is hidden and limited, temporarily abdicating from "Limitlessness," as Ein Sof - although God continues to be Ein Sof, God is suddenly Greta Garbo, "wanting to be alone."

But when we consider the nature of the Divine from the standpoint of immanence, the decision to keep a low profile makes perfect sense. Imagine that God is all there is, save for the chaos that existed before Creation.

Imagine that the "tohu wa bohu" of that primordial chaos could become something only by virtue of its relationship to that Creator. "Formless and void" may sound like nothing, but when the immanence of God is in the creative spirit, it becomes. Ayin, which translates as "I am becoming," is in the Kabbalistic model – the something that's in the process of becoming something more – the statuses do not imply non-existence. What they imply is a potential awaiting activation.

In a model of pre-existing immanence (God is present in all matter), transcendence is chosen. God, by an act of his own choosing, contracts from a status of infusing all Creation with the Divine Presence to hiding out, peeping between the blinds to make sure we're on track for the tikkun part of the festivities.

And while that sounds dire, there's much more to the story and to God's Grand Design.

Sheviroit ha Kelim

"There was spoilage for the sake of fixing and destruction for the sake of rebuilding."

Isaac Luria

In the concept of the Shevirot ha Kelim, we meet the primordial form of the sefirot. When Ein Sof attempted to conceal Ohr Ein Sof in those clay containers ("kelipot"), the clay proved unequal to the task, shattering and spilling their contents over all Creation, together with their shards. The Shevirah or "shattering" was like an experiment gone horribly wrong; a golem run amok.

In the form we see the sefirot here, they're unstable archetypes of themselves. Not yet united in the form of the Tree of Life, they're unlinked, independent entities that don't communicate and thus, shatter.

The shattering occurs in the "formless void" of tohu wa bohu, and the kelipot, those clay containers, are infected by sitra achra (evil). While the Light of the Limitless is rained down upon Creation, so are these infected shards, bearing within them the stuff of the void, tainted with evil. The effect of the juxtaposition between the Light of the Limitless and the kelipot is compelling – and yet another instance of the tension between apparent opposites or competitors.

As the question is frequently asked regarding the fruit of the Tree of Good and Evil, we must ask if Luria was not explaining something important about Creation in the quote above. Was the Shevirah "destruction for the sake of rebuilding"? Was Adam's fall? It's a worthy point of reflection for those of us theologically inclined.

The tension between good and evil co-existing in Creation through the agency of the kelipot is "spoilage for the sake of fixing," though. Because if there were no evil, no perilous way of the world offered to us, then how could it be said we choose goodness. We wouldn't have any choice but to be the ideal product God had intended to create all along.

We would not have the gift of free will – the ability to choose for ourselves which road we'll take through this wild world. Without the challenge of evil, there is no refining in the fire. There is no choice to be made.

And so, free will is living in the presence of evil and not choosing it. Having blown up something rather important in the lab, the Creator has provided us with a unique proposal – busted shards or Light of the Limitless. Busted shards of clay pots are easy enough to pick up and run off with. The Light of the Limitless, not so much. That takes character and the way of Adam Kadmon and those 613 mitzvot in the Kabbalistic model.

As the kelipot chatter, Holy Sparks – nitzotzot – are released into Creation. It's up to humanity to seek them instead of choosing to pick up those tainted shards. In Kabbalah, these Holy Sparks are sought in the performance of mitzvot. We choose to either adhere to the ephemeral nitzotzot or the material shards of kelipot, infected by sitra achra.

This is the Kabbalah's narrative of tikkun, born in the shattering of the vessels. We repair the damage done to Creation by completing the work started in the Creation of Adam.

Tikkun

Contrary to the contemporary concept of tikkun, the Kabbalistic idea of this Lurianic concept is a materialized spirituality. While the contemporary idea posits the restoration of Creation through service to one's neighbor in Creation, the Kabbalistic idea turns to physical acts rooted in the performance of mitzvot. While the goal is similar, the approach is distinctly different. And that approach is defined by Halakhah (Jewish Law).

Primordial Man, as we've read, was the realization of tikkun in God's original place. Adam Kadmon is a transcendent representation of the Garden's Adam but in his ideal, metaphysical form.

Isaac Luria believed that the work of tikkun was achieved in creating Adam – Primordial Man. But his conception of Adam Kadmon was the figure of Adam as a spiritual being of light and the direct conduit of that light.

Adam dropped the ball – well, the apple – leaving tikkun not only unrealized but unraveled.

The breaking of the vessels is like a metaphor for Adam's disobedience in the Garden. God's hopes in Adam had been dashed. His Creation had let him down spectacularly. Similarly, the Divine's hopes for the kelipot as vessels of Ohr Ein Sof was a crushing disappointment.

But isn't it true that, in both instances, God must have known? This takes us back to the quotation from Luria above. Both the shattering of the vessels and Adam's bit of the apple created a catastrophe in Creation.

Was this catastrophe planned? Because without evil, there would be no free will. But free will caused the rupture, to begin with. Adam chose to disobey, unraveling the healing of Creation in the process.

And the nitzotzot, having been released, are the Holy Sparks that emanate from the metaphysical body of Adam Kadmon, laden with the Light of the Limitless. This is our divine legacy, just as tikkun is.

Sometimes an experiment that has gone wrong shows scientists the way forward. They learn from the experience. But in the case of the Shevirot ha Kelim, it's not the scientist who must learn but those on behalf of whom the experiment was performed.

And Adam, an inspiration from the mind of God, springing forth as a sacred image, was both a monkey wrench in the works of God and an essential component. On Adam and his descendants, embodied in the prototypical Adam Kadmon, hang the Created Order's health, in the mystical work of tikkun, Isaac Luria's Kabbalistic formula for a restored Creation.

In our next chapter, we'll be discussing the Second Section of Sefer ha-Bahir, the Hebrew Alphabet. Because of Sefer ha-Bahir's nature – fragmentary and most likely produced by many authors over many periods and settings – it's most useful to discuss its contents as part of the tradition of linguistic mysticism in wider Kabbalah.

Let's turn next, then, to the alphabet and the mystical significance of Hebrew characters, vowel pointings, and choral cantillations.

Chapter Five: The Language of Creation

"Why is the letter Aleph at the beginning? Because it was before everything, even the Torah."

Sefer ha-Bahir, Section II, 17

One of the most prominent and pervasive features in Sefer ha-Bahir is that of linguistic mysticism. There is an entire section in the book – Section II, Alphabet – dedicated to mystically positioning the Hebrew language's individual characters.

There is some reference to principles of gematria in the text, but these are secondary to mystical references to the Hebrew language as an agent of Creation, its letters acting as the fabric of Creation itself while co-creating it with God. In this sense, the Hebrew language is the Language of Creation and the Language of God.

Through this section in Sefer ha-Bahir, we're treated to mystical conceptualizations of the alphabet, describing letters like Gimel in a highly physical manner, almost as one might an animal, with the letter having a tail. We also learn that the letter Bet follows Aleph because Aleph was first.

Groucho Marx might have written that one!

One of the most striking features of this section is the description of Aleph Yud and Shin's letters. Aleph is described as the head ("it was before everything"), Yod is described as "second to it," and Shin is described as including "all the world."

And here, we meet Adam in the Sefer ha-Bahir, in the guise of the Hebrew letters. The Hebrew letters Aleph, Yud, and Shin, spell the word "איש" - the Hebrew word for "man."

The Sefer ha-Bahir's mystical descriptions of Aleph and Shin's letters reveal the position of the prototype for Primordial Man in the writer's imagination, later reflected in other Kabbalistic writings. Aleph "was before everything," including Torah. This is the sequence of events we've been discussing throughout our explorations of the Creation narrative in the Kabbalistic model.

But the letter shin is the kicker in this sequence of letters, as it holds within it the totality of Creation.

With its three prongs, the letter shin resembles the graphic depiction of fire, its appearance commonly representing the "Fire of Torah." It is semiotic unto itself but a specific and potent one, readily intelligible to those who see it. Whether you know what the letter sounds like or not, you recognize the semiotic of the flames ascending.

With yud "second to" Aleph, sandwiched between it and Shin, the Hebrew character mostly commonly used to indicate the Holy Name of God (considered too Holy to speak or write by many), the yud pushes Aleph forward, the world coming up on the rear flank.

Reading Sefer ha-Bahir, the reader is variously confounded and enthralled. The sages quoted in the book disagree, talk at cross purposes - or seem to - and intersperse their remarks with wildly varied themes from the Creation narrative.

But the Hebrew alphabet's placement in the lofty position of God's creative agent is a feature, not just of Sefer ha-Bahir but of Sefer Yetzirah and the Zohar. These books, specifically, form a thematic and conceptual spine for Kabbalah and the thinking of ARI. Linguistic mysticism lives in the scroll tucked in the Golem of Prague's mouth and the ten utterances themselves. It lives, also, in the mysticism of vowel pointings, omitted from modern Hebrew but very much a part of the language's liturgical and devotional form.

And the alphabet crops up throughout Sefer ha-Bahir, outside the bounds of its designated section, making it an urgent and dominant theme in the text, demanding a discussion of its place in the greater tradition of linguistic mysticism in Judaism - Kabbalistic Judaism, especially.

In the voluptuous tradition of Jewish linguistic mysticism, the word becomes the flesh of the earth and all that is in it, as it issues from the Creator's mouth.

Speaking Creation

The Hebrew language's prominence in the Creation narrative is evident in the ten utterances that provoked God's magnum opus. But language has a much more complex role to play in the realm of Jewish Mysticism.

Gershom Scholem has written of the "reification of language," which is an apt description of linguistic mysticism. In Kabbalah, as in the Torah itself, the Hebrew language holds a special place, and that place is reified ("enfleshed") as a living part of Creation.

In Sefer, ha-Bahir are found several examples of early gematria, but little indication is given about numeric values or formulas. The linguistic mysticism of the Genesis Creation narrative is not of the same depth or systematic nature as that of the Kabbalah. This came to be developed in the late 13th Century by Abraham Abulafia (1240 –

circa 1291), who utilized the alphabet to aid in meditation toward the enlightenment of the soul.

Abulafia is considered the father of the tradition of linguistic mysticism in Kabbalah. By combining letters randomly, he eventually created a system of combining them. This led to a key component of Artificial Intelligence, called the Science of Language.

Abulafia's mission was not only to penetrate the Hebrew canon texts by rearranging letters in specific texts but to contemplate them, using a specific form of religious meditation.

His explorations led him to produce books, which were essentially compilations of proverbs constructed from his linguistic system's results. He considered these prophetic due to his mystical deployment of Hebrew characters.

This is how sages like Abulafia laid bare the "inner soul" of the texts of Torah by calling on the Hebrew language to lead them to unseen truths held within the letters' formations and sounds.

Towards the end of his life, Abulafia develops a theory of the Messiah and the redemption of Creation rooted in his mystical linguistic theories. He saw the return of the Messiah and Creation's healing in terms of the intellectual processes of devotion. The coming of the Messiah and tikkun could be achieved only through the exertions of the faithful. And even though Abulafia was considered something of a heretic, he was also a strong proponent in sharing Kabbalah widely due to his unusual methodologies. Further, he offered Judaism a new means of interpreting Messianic hope as participatory and collaborative. But perhaps, he just clarified an old idea that already existed and got lost along the way.

Living Stones

An Israeli historical philosopher of Jewish Mysticism, Moshe Idel, connects the destruction of the First and Second Temples to Scholem's reification of language. In losing the Temples, Judaism suffered two of its most painful losses.

Completed in 957 BCE, the First Temple was destroyed by the Babylonians in 586 BCE. Following the Babylonian Empire's fall in 537 BCE, the new Temple began construction the following year. (NB: this date is not considered definitive). In 70 CE, the Second Temple was destroyed during the Siege of Jerusalem by the Romans. Tradition holds that both Temples were destroyed on the same day of the year – Tisha B'Av, the ninth day of the month of Av in the Hebrew Calendar, which falls in July or August in the more commonly used Gregorian calendar.

Considered the most mournful day in the Hebrew Liturgical Calendar, Tish B'Av is also an occasion to remember other egregious wounds to the Jewish people, from the massacres of entire villages during the many Crusades which occurred in Medieval Europe to the Holocaust.

The Temple itself was constructed to replace the Tent of Meeting used by the Israelites in Sinai, which sheltered the tablets bearing the Ten Commandments. Contained in the Ark of the Covenant, both the broken set of tablets – and the one that remained whole – echo the ten utterances of the Divine in the work of Creation. The Tent of Meeting and the Temple, which replaced it, is identified as physical symbols of the Jewish People's connection to and relationship with God, having housed the Covenant made in the desert.

Now lost to history as they once stood, monuments to a people's spiritual chronology, there is nothing that can replace them or any of the religious articles they once housed. The two Temples (in reality, one) not only incarnate the relationship but stand in doleful witness – ghostly and immaterial – to the harassment of the Jews through time.

The Temple will not be rebuilt. It will not be rebuilt of stone, in any case. The Temple will be built in the hearts of the people, and the letters of the Hebrew alphabet are the stones which will build it - laid one on top of the other, in the form of the ideal Adam and guided by the mitzvot.

At least, this is how Moshe Idel conceptualizes the linguistic mysticism of Judaism, generally and Kabbalah, specifically.

No matter who the next power is to attack the Israelites, this new Temple cannot be laid siege to, sacked, or destroyed. This new Temple is inviolable and incorruptible. It has been built in the heart of the stuff of Creation - the Hebrew alphabet.

The intense reverence for language and the written word, which is such an integral part of Judaism, is the basis for its reification. In examining the Creation narrative and, specifically, the ten utterances by which Creation came to be, it's easy to follow the thematic thread, complex as it is.

Divine thought became Divine speech, forming words combined with letters. These, issuing from the mouth of God, took on the role of creative agents, building with God the Creation that, in tzimtzum, space was made for.

So, why create humanity? Why create an ideal version of humanity, to act as a cosmic partner to the process, with the Adam of the Garden, designed as the creaturely realization of that partner?

Who else has the powers of speech? Besides God, only humanity.

And so, the intimate relationship between God and Primordial Man takes on an even deeper meaning in a shared language, materialized as home, a gift from God, and as God's glory shown forth in a new and diverse way.

The living stones are shared between the Divine and Primordial Man, extending to all human life. The letters, the sounds the Divine speech releases to bring Creation into being, the words and the shared aspect of language, have all co-created - not with that Divine but as part of it. Gifted also to Primordial Man, it's that complex of linguistic mysticism that holds together Creation as a Divine Covenant.

God creates. Then, God shares, using the same breath which helped form the ten utterances to breathe life (Ruach – the Divine breath of God) into the mud doll, Adam. The intimacy of the mystical role of language in the Creation narrative and the linguistic mysticism of Kabbalah presents the idea of language as a creative force and a unifying one.

As a pretext for tikkun, the spiritualized and reified Hebrew language is inescapable. It is woven into Creation in every possible crevice, fiber, and cell. Language became part of humanity the moment God breathed life into the mud doll, in the freshness of a new Creation, constructed by Hebrew letters, conformed to the Divine Will.

In Sefer ha-Bahir's linguistic mysticism and other Kabbalistic writings, we find a personified language, providing us with all we need to mend the broken relationship between God and humanity. It's the incarnate voice of God in the living stones of Hebrew characters that point the way toward the light released at Shevirot ha Kelim and away from the shards of the tainted vessels which once contained it.

With no more resort to the Temple's ritual sacrifices, Idel's theory has prayer standing in the place of that ancient means with which to find favor with God. Prayer is language. And language is the vehicle of tikkun.

Once God created all that uses language, so the praying community deploys the same creative power to mend what has been rent asunder. This faithful re-creation of the work of the Divine at Creation thus becomes a shared project. Placing the living stones one on top of each other in community and with intention, the prayerful People reconstructs an inviolable Temple of the Spirit, impervious to all human mischief.

Prayer, interpretation, liturgy, the Holy Letters themselves – all these are agents of tikkun, in the realm of Kabbalah's linguistic mysticism. Language, as the Divinely gifted tool, is formed to the Will of the Creator. It rises like incense to the concealed God, healing Creation as it drifts upward and pleasing the Limitless, limited for our sakes in tzimtzum.

Hebrew – Mother Language

That Hebrew is spoken today by only about 9 million people fails to recognize the tremendous impact it's had on the languages we speak today. This impact is commensurate with that of Latin and Ancient Greek.

The Lashon HaKodesh, or holy language, lay extinct as a living, public language for 2,000 years. Finally revived only 150 years ago, it lurked in Holy Books and Torah scrolls and in the prayers of the faithful. It never died. It just hid between the pages of books and in the prayers of Jews.

Much of the devaluation of the Hebrew language's influence on Western Civilization is due to the compartmentalization of cultures existing in the Ancient Near East. This is primarily due to the ascension of Christianity, which emphasizes the primacy of Greece and Rome.

This emphasis ignores the establishment of monotheism as a norm in Western Civilization, the contribution of Judeo-Christian ethics to laws within that context, and the alphabet (alphabet) itself. Part of the problem is the annexation of regional cultures by the Roman Empire and identifying these cultures as "Western" due to that process of annexation.

We've already touched on Hellenism's heavy influence on Jewish thought, which endured until at least the 11th Century. It's probably impossible to discuss Judaism or other religiously-motivated cultural expressions of the region and time without noting a great deal of cross-pollination. The Ancient Near East was a melting pot created by waves of invasions, sieges, and Imperial colonization.

But Hebrew is considered by many to be the Mother of all languages. This is true in Judaism due to its mystical role in Creation, whether through Genesis or the Kabbalistic writings about it.

Whether this can be proven linguistically or only spiritually, the Hebrew language, which finds its closest living relative in Arabic, has a graphic quality that lends itself to mystical pursuits.

Elegant - and at times, even expository - the letter shin, for example, with its three prongs, resembling tongues of flame - the Hebrew alphabet letters have an almost ferocious quality in their classical form. They attract while frustrating those looking at them who cannot interpret what their entrancing forms mean.

Originally existing as a system called "abjad," the Hebrew alphabet consisted of only consonants, with the letters aleph, hey, vav, and yud acting as mediators to create vowels by forming combinations with other letters.

But niqqud, the Hebrew linguistic system of "pointings," creates vowel sounds in this language of consonants. Pointings usually appear below the consonant, with one exception of a pointing written above the consonant and two freestanding vowels.

Most modern Hebrew omits pointings, using ktiv male - without pointings. Pointings are usually reserved for children's books (as they're learning) and Holy texts (as pointings have meaning and are considered traditional). But the niqqud system only goes back to about 600 CE, when it began to be added to existing Bibles by the Masoretes. These scribes' work continued until the early part of the 15th Century - a period of more than 700 hundred years.

The Masoretes of Tiberias developed the system of pointings used today. The Masoretes developed the system of cantillation, indicating cadence for chanting/singing Holy Scripture and as for punctuation. We'll talk more about them in the next section.

But cantillations in Hebrew texts also serve an interpretative role.

Cantillations are used to mark Bible verses into what amount thematic chunks. This effect is often achieved using signs indicating that certain words should become a single, impactful phrase. In this usage, cantillation signs most resemble modern punctuation.

Cantillation signs also help in determining the emphasis in any given word toward correct pronunciation.

When applied to music, cantillation signs create a chant of Scripture, also emphasizing the syllables in individual words as a type of rhythmic device while following the correct pronunciation and emphasis.

Deeper

"He said to them: Come and hear the fine points regarding the vowel points found in the Torah of Moses."

Sefer ha-Bahir, Section IV, 42

While we recognize the spiritual aspect of the letters of the Hebrew alphabet, what do the pointings and cantillations mean in this mystical scheme?

Niqqud is considered to have a deeper meaning than even the letters. In Kabbalah, the pointings and cantillations are viewed as having the same function of the soul to the body. They express the inner truth of the letters. Providing a pleasing shape to the language, the niqqud almost serves the Divine breath's purpose in the otherwise rigid, forthright world of consonants, enlivening them with their full nature and purpose.

The Kabbalists believe that the soul is the life of the living body and that the niqqud corresponds to that corporeal purpose by providing the same function to the Hebrew alphabet.

While innovation in the life of the language, appearing only after the Common Era, it's clear that the niqqud has found a role in the linguistic mysticism of Kabbalah, enlivening and enriching it with yet another layer of esoteric meaning. While not extant for millennia and now banished to sacred texts and easy reading volumes for youngsters, the markings which define holy writings have their own esoteric meaning, sharing it with the alphabet in a rich dance of graphic representations celebrating Creation.

As unseen as the human soul is to the greater world, the pointings and cantillations in sacred Hebrew texts bear traces of essential meaning. They accompany the letters they adhere to, bearing Creation's burden, as they join in the dance.

And in Sefer ha-Bahir, references to pointings and cantillations indicate later glosses to the text, as these didn't appear in the Hebrew language until the 7th Century CE, as stated above. But with Sefer ha-Bahir, this fractured product of multiple hands and many ages, that is no surprise.

The Masoretes

Centered in Tiberius, Jerusalem, and even in Babylonia, the Masoretes were groups of scribes working together to create a system that could universalize pronunciation and grammar in the Hebrew Scriptures. To do this, they created diacritical notes – the pointings and cantillations we're talking about. These markings acted as learned recommendations about how the text was to be said or sung.

Known as the "keepers of tradition," the Masoretes systematically and arduously created a universal system to standardize pronunciations. This was a sacred and much-needed undertaking due to the nature of an adqab language. A string of consonants might express more than one meaning; more than one thought.

The work of the Masoretes in creating the system of pointings and cantillations was interactive, demanding these learned scholars and scribes engage with the text and allow it to speak. In this is the true mystical nature of the niqqud.

Imagine the human intellect meeting the text as it stood to give it a voice that might be understood in precisely the same way by whoever might read it. The ambiguity of a language consisting solely of consonants was overcome by these 7th to 10th Century scribes and their life's work – to give the Hebrew Scriptures their true voice.

Maybe I'm too romantic for my own good, but doesn't that sound rather like tikkun to you? Not to imply that the Hebrew language is broken. Rather, it suggests that dedicated human hands enhanced the Hebrew Scriptures and their Holy Language's clarity. They were enhanced to be more readily understood through the intellectual and spiritual magic of cantillations and pointings.

As ARI once said, "There was spoilage for the sake of fixing." Perhaps this is true of the Hebrew language. Perhaps it's true of that broken set of tablets carried through the desert in the Ark of the Covenant. In God's world, things are broken for good reason. As humanity is called to address that brokenness, it re-learns the lessons it was once created knowing. All of it rejected for the sake of a snack.

Whatever the truth is, it must be acknowledged that the tremendous accomplishment of the Masoretes is to be recognized as a service to the Hebrew language. That accomplishment was pursued for over 700 years. This level of devotion to Scripture's integrity, involving innumerable scholars and scribes and resulting in a standardized text, seems almost mythical. But it happened. And because of that devotion, the Hebrew language, while changing in modern times in its popular, Israeli form – as all languages do – maintained its integrity over two millennia of not being uttered in conversation as a living language.

In our next chapter, we'll be revisiting the sefirot, described in Sefer ha-Bahir, which has seven voices and three sayings. Let's find out what's intended by this claim.

Chapter Six: The Seven Voices and the Sefirot

"It is the glory of God to conceal things."

Proverbs 25: 2a

Just when you thought you knew as much as you would ever know about the sefirot, along comes Sefer ha-Bahir to prove you wrong.

Its treatment of the sefirot and what they mean to the Creation narrative is of great interest, as in this work, they take on the role of Divine speech.

Section II of the Sefer ha-Bahir is entitled 'The Seven Voices and the Sefirot.' I'm sure several of you are asking why there are only seven voices and not ten. The answer – there are also three sayings that correspond to the sefirot in the text's model. These are called amarim.

Let's get started on the Sefer ha-Bahir vision of the sefirot by drilling down to the seven voices' origin.

Seeing Voices

A hymn of praise for the God of Creation, Psalm 29 relates the power and glory of the voice of the Creator, repeating seven times the phrase, "The voice of the LORD." These are the seven voices "all the people saw," according to Sefer ha-Bahir, at Mt. Horeb (Exodus 20: 18-19).

What the people saw at Mt. Horeb was a theophany – a manifestation of God in "thunder and lightning, the sound of the trumpet and the mountain smoking" (Exodus 20: 18a). In the NRSV, the word "witnessed" refers to the thunder and lightning, smoke, and trumpet experienced by the people.

But in the original Hebrew, the phrase used translates as "they saw the voices." Many translations of this verse are similar to that seen in the NRSV. The phenomenon of theophany is witnessed or perceived, but the spectacle is referred to by its constituent parts. All those parts are creaturely phenomena, in the eyes of the onlooker.

There is a quality to the description that signals what it is, even if the Hebrew translations fail to capture the supernatural nature of what the people witnessed, perceived, or saw.

Can you see a sound? Air horns, gunshots, fireworks, and other extraordinary aural manifestations can all seem that way, sometimes. But we're talking about an entirely different kind of seeing - and hearing - in the Exodus verse.

In the presence of the Holy One, so near and yet so far, the people are terrified. That the God they're entering into Covenant with might be so extravagant in manifesting Divine Glory has them shaking in their boots. They have seen but what they have seen has no form. Their senses have been scrambled by the mystical theophany of God, in celebration of Covenant and as a display of Divine Power.

Theophany amounts to a direct experience of God and a manifestation of Divine Power. The idea is the Ancient Hebrew version of "shock and awe." The people experience theophany as a spectacle, intended to make it clear which side their bread is buttered on and further, to make abundantly clear the consequences of dropping that bread on the ground, butter side down.

You probably wouldn't want to meet a God who made such a shockingly visible racket, and neither did the people wandering around with Moses in the Sinai. They stood far away as Moses entered the billowing, cacophonous cloud which concealed the frightening – and inordinately loud – God of Israel.

Synesthesia is one way of seeing how it was that the creaturely senses of the Israelites were scrambled. This condition leads to concurrent experiences of sensory phenomena in disparate senses – for example, you see something that you hear. You hear something that you see. So, what's being said in the original Hebrew is that people experienced what might be called mystical or spiritual synesthesia as a reaction to the theophany they were experiencing.

Sefer ha-Bahir takes this one step further, saying that the people did, indeed, see God in witnessing the "thunder and lightning." In the Hebrew original, the word hakolot is used, which is "thunders." This is explained in Shemot Rabbah 5:9, which references Rabbi Yochanan ben Zakkai's (1st Century CE) theory that the sound of God's voice was heard in all the languages of the earth, creating a type of thunder. "Thunders" is pointed out as the sound made by the Divine Voice simultaneously transmitting the guidelines of the Covenant to the people in all extant languages. According to Rabbi Yochanan, these were 70 in number.

But Sefer ha-Bahir also points out (in stanza 47) that in Deuteronomy 4:15, Moses tells the people that they "saw no form" when God spoke to them at Horeb "out of the fire." The same stanza reminds readers that in Deuteronomy 4:12, "a voice of words you heard."

The stanza employs the King's analogous figure again, suggesting that it continues to be audible when the King's voice is far away. So, while there is a separation between God and the theophany provoked by God, there's a parallel sensory experience in witnesses to it that both conceals and reveals the Divine source of the spectacle.

The seven voices are the manifestation of God at Mt. Horeb, demonstrating Divine Power. In casting the sefirot as the seven voices, Sefer ha-Bahir directly relates them to the voice of God – a voice which emanates in 70 languages simultaneously, creating "thunders."

The voice/voices emanate(s) from the Divine just as the sefirot do and just as the seven voices of David's hymn of praise, Psalm 29, do. What's being intimated is the presence of the sefirot in all the works of God, beginning with creation and continuing at Mt. Horeb, as expressed in Psalm 29:3, "The voice of the LORD is over the waters; the God of glory thunders, the LORD, over mighty waters," just as "God swept over the face of the waters" in Genesis 1: 2. The same verse reminds us that "The voice of the LORD is powerful, the voice the LORD is full of majesty."

And so, the seven voices, speaking to the majesty of the Divine, stand as emanations, in whatever situation they're found. Both emanating from the Divine and intrinsically part of whatever God is, the sefirot were born on the Divine breath in Sefer ha-Bahir, processing the Holy One's attributes into Creation and to all who live in its precincts.

The Amarim

In the second half of stanza 49, we meet the three amarim or sayings. Again, these are derived from the Hebrew Scriptures and explained in the text.

The scriptures implicated in the discernment of the amarim are found in stanza 49, beginning with Deuteronomy 26: 18, "Today the LORD has obtained your agreement: to be his treasured people, as he promised you, and to keep his commandments."

Proverbs 4: 7 follows in the text, saying, "The beginning of wisdom is this: get wisdom, and whatever else you get, get insight."

Job 32: 8 follows, which says, "But truly it is the spirit in a mortal, the breath of the Almighty, that makes for understanding."

Stanza 49 of Section III ends with a summation of the information in the three Hebrew Scripture verses, saying, "As the old man said to the child, "What is hidden from you, do not seek, and what is concealed from you, do not probe. Where you have authority, seek to understand, but you have nothing to do with mysteries."

This is a paraphrase from the Book of Sirach, which appears in the Deuterocanonical or Apocryphal books. To clarify the thought, the scripture concerned (Sirach 3: 21-23) reads:

"Neither seek what is too difficult for you nor investigate what is beyond your power. Reflect upon what you have been commanded, for what is hidden is not your concern. Do not meddle in matters that are beyond you, for more than you can understand has been shown you."

Beginning with a timely reminder that God has ordained Israel as his chosen (treasured) people, the people are reminded of the Divine Covenant they've entered, delineated by the mitzvot (commandments). The work of humanity in approaching the Divine toward reconciliation is also circumscribed by the three sayings, which are summed up in the metaphor of the old man and the child.

Within that framework, Proverbs 4: 7 advises that humanity is to "get wisdom," but that wisdom must be supported by insight to have meaning. The verse implies that the getting of wisdom is just the beginning, with insight guiding the obtained ability to understand. This implies that insight is the foundation of wisdom and its intellectual launch pad.

Finally, we find in Job 32:8 that humanity's ability to understand exists only by virtue of the Divine breath that animated it at Creation. It is the Ruach borne in each human that enlivens the human intellect – not the individual's intellectual virtue. In this model, the human intellect is a gift extended to the mud doll in the Garden by the Creator's breath.

These three sayings – that humans (Israel, specifically) are bound in an everlasting Covenant with God, that getting wisdom is part of that Covenant, guided by insight, and finally, that it's by the grace of the Divine breath that humans can "understand."

Wisdom in Sefer ha-Bahir, framed as a gift which we're obliged to employ, is also limited in the human intellect, as described in the metaphor of the old man and the child. The paraphrase of Sirach clarifies that, while the Covenant between God and humanity is to be lived out in pursuit of wisdom and understanding that "more than (we) can understand has been shown (us)

As created beings, our intellects are limited. We are not the Divine Creator. However, we bear in us the image of God through the animating Divine breath.

But what is meant by that final phrase in the old man/child parable?

If you'll recall, Adam was created with all he needed to know infused in him. He was, in fact, the realization of tikkun at Creation. More than he could understand had been shown him. By breaking faith and partaking of the forbidden fruit, Adam broke tikkun, and the vessels shattered, littering Creation with the pollution of evil.

And so, the three sayings point to tikkun as the work of the sefirot, beyond being the voice of God. They are not only the voices of Psalm 29, as described by David; they are the living Covenant, as well as emissaries and guides in the elevation of humanity to its full spiritual potential. While the operation of the sefirot as emanations of God is unlimited, humanity's is not. Originally limitless, embodying healing and the Created Order's stewardship, Adam, the finished product, took a nosedive, leaving the rest of mystical Israel to clean up the shevirot ha kelim.

Within our creaturely framework, humanity has much to contribute. In essence, the sefirot in Sefer ha-Bahir are operating as the seven voices. But they also take on a didactic role in the three sayings, reminding mystical Israel of its agreement with God, urging the faithful to obtain wisdom accompanied by insight, then reminding them that their intellects are limited by the fall of Adam but retained by the grace of the Divine breath.

Hester Panim

In this section of Sefer ha-Bahir, the sefirot take on their role as both voices of God and teachers. As emanations of the Divine, they are teaching us the way toward tikkun.

I started this chapter with part of a verse from the Book of Proverbs to highlight the idea of concealment extant in the Seven Voices and the sefirot. This theme is important in Jewish mystical thought, as we've seen in the Bible texts above, which tie the section together.

Concealment is a recurring theme throughout the Hebrew Scriptures. In Christianity, the concealment of God appears on the day following the Crucifixion of Christ. Roman Catholics and Anglicans/Episcopalians believe that Christ descended to Hell before his resurrection to release the souls of the righteous. On this day, God is said to have been "concealed." The altars of these denominations' churches are stripped bare on Maundy Thursday (Agony in the Garden in the Gospel of John) and remain unadorned until the Holy Saturday mass, timed to celebrate the Resurrection for midnight on Saturday/Sunday when Christ is resurrected.

But in Jewish Mysticism, tzimtzum is the home of this concealed God, awaiting Creation's healing. In this model, the sefirot process God into Creation, speaking tikkun into being the voices and teachers of God.

And Sefer ha-Bahir is a primary source for this cosmology of breaking, concealment, and pursuing wisdom as a necessary tool of tikkun. While the role it presents the sefirot in is not the well-developed, systematic explanation we see in later Kabbalah, the nature of the sefirot in this primary form is the basis for later development.

Before we leave this discussion, let's look at the full text of Proverbs 25:2, which reads, "It is the glory of God to conceal things, but the glory of kings is to search things out."

Let's illuminate this text with Deuteronomy 29:29, which reads, "The secret things belong to the LORD our God, but the revealed things belong to us and our children forever, to observe all the words of this law."

While Sefer ha-Bahir draws on the texts of Hebrew Scripture to illustrate humanity's purpose in God's Creation, it applies an esoteric context. Reminding readers, on the one hand, to seek wisdom ("to observe all the words of this law") it also warns of creaturely overreach and that God is concealed to be sought but not necessarily known in the fullness of all God is ("seek what is too difficult for you").

The hester panim, the hidden face of God, is not what is being sought. As the people at Mt. Horeb discovered, it was hidden for a good reason, being a terrible and awe-inspiring reality. But the wisdom to understand and adhere to the Covenant is what humanity has been enjoined to perform. And while Jewish Mysticism seeks the hester panim, it does so through the satisfaction of the mitzvot.

In concert with the seven voices and the amarim that adhere to them, the sefirot reveals only what we need to know to "get wisdom." In that wisdom is the way to tikkun and the hester panim.

And if we scratch the Sefer ha-Bahir in the right place – which is this section - we see that it's repeating the ancient direction of Proverbs 1: 7, namely that "The fear of the LORD is the beginning of knowledge; fools despise wisdom and instruction."

In other words, if you know what's good for you, you'll "get wisdom," toe the line and understand your human limitations in the face of a fearsome Deity.

Chapter Seven: The Name Game

"You shall not make wrongful use of the name of the LORD your God, for the LORD will not acquit anyone who misuses his name."

Exodus 20: 7

Prominent in Sefer ha-Bahir is the Tetragrammaton (YHVH) as the name of God. This is the Name employed throughout the Hebrew Scriptures, occurring in every book of that canon, save Esther and Ecclesiastes. There is only one possible instance in the Song of Solomon in the Apocrypha, but this is most likely translated simply as "yah," which differs from the Tetragrammaton.

While "yah" might be considered shorthand for YHVH, it is not the ineffable name any more convincingly than when it's cryptically expressed as the letter yud or the letters yud and hey. Shorthand for God in writing and speech is to satisfy the Holy Name concept is too holy to either record or speak. This Jewish practice follows not only the Commandment that God's Name should not be taken in vain but reminds the faithful of the holiness of God. It's instructive to think of the Tetragrammaton in these intramural terms when talking about the Name of God and the theme of the complete "otherness of the Divine Creator."

It should be noted, following our discussion of concealment and the hester panim, that the absence of the Tetragrammaton in the Book of Esther furthers the theme of God's concealment in that narrative.

Esther's story describes the salvation of the Jewish people from a genocide at the hands of the Persians. In the end, Esther becomes Queen and saves her people. This is the origin story of the Festival of Purim. But what's unique about the book is the apparent absence of the Tetragrammaton.

The truth, though, is something entirely different. The Holy Name is there. It's just not there in its usual format. It is expressed in the text of Esther via Hebrew acrostics. The acrostic form is not found in most languages, usually occurring in either English or German.

An acrostic uses a formula in which either the first or last letters of a four-word phrase are used to compose a word that otherwise isn't seen in any given text – YHVH. There are four instances of the Tetragrammaton in the Book of Esther, spelling the Holy Name both backward and forward (Esther 1:17; 1:20; 5:4; 5:13; and 7:.7).

This device highlights the theme of God's concealment and the role of humanity in seeking reconciliation with God through fervently seeking the Divine.

And with Esther, in the Persian world into which she and other Jews had assimilated, reconciliation was surely needed. It was that very secularized and assimilated expression of Judaism that the Israelites were warned of in Deuteronomy 31: 18, which says, "On that day I will surely hide my face on account of all the evil they have done by turning to other gods."

Even in Esther's name, we find the concealed God, as Hebrew scholars understand it, to be a way of disguising the phrase "haster astir panai" or "concealed God."

And so, the Holy Name is cleverly hidden in Esther, but it's in the text for those who are equipped to "get wisdom."

The hidden God as a central theme in the Exodus narrative has been indelibly impressed upon and actively developed in Kabbalistic traditions. The Sefer ha-Bahir's Biblically rooted parables are thus served as a mystical exegesis that illuminates Torah, standing as its soul.

The Tetragrammaton in Sefer ha-Bahir

YHVH appears in the text of Sefer ha-Bahir 19 times, but there are several interpretations of what the Holy Name conveys in that setting, with four presenting as critical.

In the first of these, the Holy Name is presented as a means for believers to be guided in prayer, leading their devotions toward tikkun. In the second, YHVH is aligned with one of the sefirot. This is usually tiferet/beauty, at the center of Etz Chaim, rendering the Holy Name a didactic device and, thus, a key facet of Divinity (remembering the sefirot's teaching role as emanations of God, in the amarim). The third interpretation present in the work is that of a roadmap to the sefirot, investing each letter of the Tetragrammaton with a specific purpose. Finally, YHVH is interpreted as being the fullness of the Torah, opening the Holy Name to a world of interpretative possibilities.

When these four interpretations are united, the Tetragrammaton stands as a graphic depiction of the Divine, representing, defining, and expressing the ineffability of God, only penetrable by way of devotion.

Historical and Biblical Context

Following the Exile in Babylon (6th Century BCE), but more precisely, starting in the 3rd Century BCE, the name "Yahweh" stopped being used. While this name continues to be associated with the Tetragrammaton in some religious circles (namely conservative Christian ones), the proper pronunciation, according to the later Masoretic vowel pointings, would have been "yeh vey").

At this point in the Hebrew people's story, Judaism was flourishing, spreading outward and becoming less localized. To acknowledge this reality, the name Elohim began to be used. This was a rejection of henotheism (the belief that one god is better than other gods in the region) and a resounding endorsement of monotheism – even though "Elohim" is a plural name. Perhaps it's the plurality, though; that's the point. In the plurality is the majesty and grandeur of God.

The word also co-opts the Canaanite usage, describing their system of multiple deities arranged in a hierarchical pantheon. The intimation is that the God of Israel is the One True God, subsuming all other gods within the reality of the Only God.

But the origin of the Divine Name, YHVH, is rooted in Scripture, namely, Exodus 3: 13 – 15, in which Moses asks God his name. The response reflects ineffability when God replies, from within the flames of the burning bush in verse 14: "I AM WHO I AM."

Related to the Hebrew verb "to be," the Tetragrammaton encompasses past, present, and future, containing all three tenses of the verb:

Present: "ho-vey"

Past: "hay-ya"

Future: "yay-hay-yay"

By claiming for the Divine the limitless expanse of time itself, the transcendence of God is highlighted. God encompasses and contains within Godhead time's vastness as definitions. In his meeting with Moses, God has refused to be named in the conventional way we regard names. Rather, the Divine has beat around the burning bush by telling Moses that God is, God was, and God will be.

That ineffability also reflects the Ancients' idea that naming something or someone changed the power dynamic. God's naming of the sun and moon in the Genesis Creation story (Genesis 1: 16 – 18) is notable due to the pagan practice of worshiping these heavenly bodies as deities. In naming them "greater light" and "lesser light," these creaturely elements are put in their places in a new Creation.

In refusing to be defined by a name but by time itself, God makes it clear in this superficial-sounding avoidance tactic that the question is impudent. God doesn't answer questions that creatures in God's Creation shouldn't be asked – at least not yet. And God is time itself, beyond being bound to any name. Names, in the traditional sense, are not for the Divine. They're for creatures.

Evidence of the Tetragrammaton's circulation as early as 850 BCE is shown in the Moabite Stone. This artifact was found near the Dead Sea and recounted the victories of the Moabite King, Mesha, against the Israelites.

Because of the nature of the encounter in which God was revealed to Moses in the burning bush, the Holy Name in the form of the Tetragrammaton became associated with God's ineffability and humanity's delicacy in the face of that "unknowableness." God will not be pinned down, and so, to honor that "evasiveness," Jews used the letters "vav hey" or "vav" or sometimes, just a dot to indicate the Divine Name. Too holy be written and too fearsome to be spoken aloud, YHVH's sacred nature is acknowledged in refraining from speaking or writing it.

In prayer and worship, "Adonai" (another plural name, meaning "my Lords" is substituted, while in daily life, "ha shem" (literally, the name) is used. This practice applies, not just to the Tetragrammaton, but to all the seven names of God: Eloah (God), El (God), Shaddai (Almighty), Tzevaot (of hosts), and Ehyeh (I am).

The Explicit Name

The Explicit Name of God is discussed in Sefer ha-Bahir in stanza 111, in Section 5, Mysteries of the Soul. In Hebrew, Shem ha Mephorash, the Explicit Name, is a term forwarded by the Tannaitic scribes, the Tannaim.

Tannaim meanings, "repeaters" or "teachers." These were the early sages who formulated the texts of the Mishnah, from 10 through 220 CE. What's intended is that God's hidden name in Kabbalah is explicit in its power and inviolability.

Here is where the Sefer ha-Bahir gets numerical. The name may have 4, 12, 22, 42, or 72 letters. The Tetragrammaton is, of course, the 4-letter name, while the 12-letter, 22-letter, and 42-letter names are much less clear and prominent.

Maimonides' interpretation of Shem ha Mephorash was that it applied only to YHVH. And the 12-letter variant comprises three mentions of the Tetragrammaton in the Aaronic or Priestly Blessing/Benediction (see below).

The 22-letter version is seen in the Sefer Raziel haMalakh (Book of the Angel Raziel, 13th Century), but not interpreted, with the transliterated name reading "Anaktim Pastam Paspasim Dionsim." This variant is mysterious but has precedents in the Geonic period (late 6th Century – mid-11th Century CE) of the Babylonian scribes. This means it predates the Book of the Angel Raziel. Regardless, there is no agreement on the language it's derived from.

Ha Gaon (939 – 1038 CE) wrote of the 42-letter version of the Name, saying there is no direction (through pointings) about pronunciation. But the general agreement on this variant is that it was produced by combining the opening 42 letters of the Book of Genesis. This variant is also found in Sefer Raziel ha Malakh.

The 72-fold name is the flashiest of the variants of the Explicit Name, having once been employed by Moses to part the Red Sea (Exodus 14: 19 – 21), according to a variety of Kabbalists. This version of the Name is also prominent in Sefer Raziel.

This version of the name is intended to be read as a boustrophedon (text which reads left to right, then right to the left in alternating lines). Read in this manner; the Explicit Name is said to have the power to exorcise demons, heal, prevent catastrophes, and dispatch one's enemies, if necessary.

The name is also an amulet of protection, as seen in Exodus 28: 36 – 38, when the name of God was sealed on Aaron's forehead, as he was created a priest or Cohen. In this amulet was the protection of the people of Israel, with Aaron taking "on himself any guilt incurred in the holy offering that the Israelites consecrate as their sacred donations" (Exodus 28: 38a). Through this act, the name is concurrently placed on the people of Israel, as stated in Numbers 6: 27, "So they shall put my name on the Israelites, and I will bless them."

In this manner, Aaron becomes the scapegoat of Leviticus 16: 6 – 9, taking responsibility for the collective errors of the people, yet protected in that role by the Holy Name.

The text of Sefer ha-Bahir then refers to the Aaronic Blessing in Numbers 6: 24-26, "The LORD bless you and keep you, the LORD make his face to shine upon you, and be gracious to you; the LORD lift up his countenance upon on you – and give you peace."

The stanza refers to Numbers 6:27, in which the Holy Name is placed upon Israel as a blessing. In the Aaronic Blessing are three instances of the Tetragrammaton, each having four letters and adding up to 12 to form the 12-letter variant of the Name.

And of these 12 letters, in Stanza 112, appear 12 Holy Names, each of them for 1 of the 12 Tribes of Israel. There follows a description of the Tribes as "12 rods", playing on the fact that the root for the word "shevet," in Hebrew, is the same for both "tribe" and "rod."

What's in a Name? *"The Tao that can be told is not the eternal Tao; the name that can be named is not the eternal name."*

Tao Te Ching, verse 1

Meaning "way," Tao (also "Dao) is central to many Asian philosophies, especially in China. While it might seem odd to you that we're suddenly discussing Tao and the contents of the Tao Te-Ching, the parallels to the Hebrew concept of the Holy Name should be apparent.

While Sefer ha-Bahir and the Kabbalah of which it's the foundation have traditionally stood slightly toward the fringe of Judaism, it's clear that the revelations of Kabbalistic thinking have found their way home in many sectors of modern Judaism. But the mysticism of a God who will not be named extends to cultures around the world.

And the name YHWH – a refusal to be bound by a name – is an example in this global, mystical tradition. Sefer ha-Bahir is part of that tradition of illuminating the darkness – even in its name. The brilliance of Sefer ha-Bahir can be seen in its cryptic style – expository in some ways and secretive in others. Intended for the eyes only of those prepared to penetrate its lessons, it's most certainly not an easy read. But the concepts expressed in its exploration of Shem ha Mephoresh and the Tetragrammaton are worth the effort.

The parables of the Bahir piece together and further flesh out the texts of Hebrew Scripture, realizing an expanded lexicon for the original scribes and a more complex lens through which to see the story of God's name.

In the story of Moses asking God's name, we see an innocent creature not yet accustomed to god's being completely beyond human thought. While we can approach the cloud, most of us are unwilling to enter it. And perhaps that hesitancy is some unknown inner knowledge of God's refusal to be named or fully known.

Chapter Eight: More on the Sefirot

"The LORD, the LORD, a God merciful and gracious."
Exodus 34: 6

In Section IV of Sefer ha-Bahir, the book again turns to the Sefirot to further instruct on their nature and work in Creation. We'll start with an examination of the relationship between wisdom and glory. Wisdom is a major theme in Sefer ha-Bahir, with the word and explanations of its meaning appearing throughout.

The section begins with a discussion of the verse from Exodus above, describing God's mercy and graciousness.

The discussion then turns to Isaiah 6:3, "Holy, Holy, Holy is the LORD of hosts; the whole earth is full of his glory."

The text of the Bahir then breaks the words "Holy, Holy, Holy" down:

- The first "Holy" represents the Crown (Keter).
- The second "Holy" is "the root of the Tree" - Foundation (Yesod).
- The third "Holy" is "attached and unified in them all" - the sefirot.

• The status of the third "Holy" is then clarified in another story about the analogous King.

The explanation employs the figures of sons and grandsons, saying that when the King's grandsons are doing what the King wants them to do, he gives them whatever they want through their sons. But when the grandsons aren't following orders, he stops providing for the grandsons.

In this analogy, we can see that God is the father of the "sons" (sefirot) and the grandsons (Covenanted humanity). When humans don't do the Creator's will, only the sefirot are fed with the attributes and voices of God and the Divine mandate to seek wisdom (up to a certain point) via the amarim.

Section IV, named the ten Sephirot, is by no means a challenge to the Seven Voices Section. Rather, it's an embellishment, offering a further interpretative channel by employing different metaphors and connections to scripture. It should also be remembered that various writers contributed to Sefer ha-Bahir over an expanse of time and text.

The concept of glory is explored at length in this section as part of a Mishnaic examination of Isaiah 6:3. The initial phase of that glory's meaning is that of Creation on the first day, casting Creation as parallel to the Land of Israel.

Glory is then characterized as "wisdom," following Proverbs 3: 35, which reads (in the original Hebrew, while the English word "honor" is used in the NRSV, which is a Hebrew synonym) "The wise will inherit glory."

Here, we should consider the properties of glory and its stated relationship to wisdom. In this section, Sefer ha-Bahir's authors chose to incarnate glory as a woman in the service of a master with many sons. Her sons visit and are told they can't see her at that moment.

But they bless her, wherever she is. Having been invested with the wisdom of the "mother" (cast as an analogy to glory), they accept that they will see her when the time comes, as they humbly (and wisely) accept that their understanding is limited, so glory is not available to them - yet.

Wisdom and glory are intimately related, recurring throughout the Sefir ha-Bahir in numerous ways. Because we're talking about a foundational text for Kabbalah and because the sefirot are central to that canon, it's important to remember that Sefer ha-Bahir is fragmentary and disjointed. The document we encounter in the Aryeh Kaplan translation is that same disjointed document, and so, the discussion of the sefirot in relation to other Biblical principles and "magic" numbers, punctuated by numerous parallels and analogies, may seem unfamiliar. But the themes of wisdom and glory are pivotal to this work and the Hebrew Scripture presented in its pages, and so, we'll discuss these attributes to further illuminate the philosophical standpoint of the text.

Defining Glory Through Wisdom

The Hebrew Scriptures speak extensively of the Glory of God. In Hebrew, glory is "kavod," with "honor" as a synonym, together with "respect" and "majesty." But the word has also been translated as meaning "weight" or "heaviness."

Divine Glory can be a lot of things - whatever it will be. It can be Ezekiel's chariot and the smoke and cacophony of Mt. Horeb or Moses before the burning bush. It can be as undramatic as a sensation of wholeness or gratitude. God's glory, then, might well be in the kind of wisdom instructed by the three amarim.

Glory is humanity's perspective on God's manifestation and revelation in the Created Order. The birth of a child, a tsunami, a rainbow, a seagull. All these are manifestations, but the truth about God's glory is that something unusual is usually going on.

Smoke! Trumpets! Fire! Flaming bushes that talk! Now, those are manifestations!

And so is wisdom. Wisdom in the human mind is a mysterious demonstration of the uniqueness of the brains with which we've been gifted. These brains can do incredible things, as evidenced in the story of the Sefer ha-Bahir. Humans had Biblical interpretations and Kabbalistic angles they wanted to share with other faithful people, and so they wrote about them, growing their spiritual understanding as they did. Later generations built on and subsumed the original, less-developed ideas, building a massive complex of religious, philosophical thought on its very bare-bones, reifying its complex themes, and filling in its many blanks.

And now, you're sitting here reading about it. You're reading a book about other books, drilling down to see what you can derive from its themes to grow your knowledge or spirituality or term paper.

Are you ignoring the magical formula of the Amarim? Are you getting greedy about "getting wisdom?" No. You're fulfilling a role that's always been intended for you since before the Creation of Primordial Man, metaphysically embodied by mystical Adam Kadmon, the prototype of humanity's full flowering. According to Kabbalah, if you're reading this, you're probably smart enough to know your limits – especially if you've read the other two books in this series.

Glory is wisdom, as wisdom is glory. Processing from the heart of God as the sefirah, Chochmah, wisdom also represents the right brain in the human body; the Etz Chaim/Adam Kadmon. And while the Kabbalists of the earliest layer of Jewish Mysticism could not have known this, nor those of the Middle Ages or even the 18th Century, they might be surprised to know that the right brain is the artistic, creative side of the brain. It's the left brain that governs items like logic, linear thinking, and computation.

But wisdom can't be described as any of those functions, much less solely associated with the empirical. Wisdom is something much more than that, so what can we derive from wisdom being associated with the brain's right side and the creative bent associated with it?

First, we must understand that the right brain also governs intuition and imagination. Right-brained thinkers are more willing to listen to what their inner voice says about whatever the world presents to them. They're also more willing to apply an imaginative response to problems and challenges.

Wisdom and intelligence are closely related. It's probably most proper to say that intelligence is where wisdom finds its potential. But intelligence is, by no means, the sum total of wisdom.

Wisdom is the glory of minds that utilize more than the usual 10% capacity most humans employ during their lifetimes. Wisdom is intellect processed through more than one filter, which confronts truths with boldness, enquiring, learning, and applying a growth model to the intellectual riches most of us call on so parsimoniously.

Wisdom is glory when intentionally and devotedly pursued, especially when that wisdom is directed toward tikkun. When wisdom increases, the manifestation of God's Glory increases. There is a cosmic connection between these two realities - one creaturely, the other Divine - which amounts to a partnership. This was intended for Adam in the Garden.

We're all familiar with the story at this point. Wisdom, though, is a story still being told by the cleanup crew, refreshed each day in its pursuit by the Glory of God indwelling limited human wisdom toward the healing of a cherished relationship.

Defining Wisdom Through the Glory

Wisdom is a creative agent in both the right brain sense and that of tikkun. Repairs are part of any system. Corrections are needed to ensure that the integrity of the structure is not threatened. Tension is employed to keep everything in its place, but in Olam Habah, the World to Come, all tension is resolved.

We've read that the right brain is adept in artistic expression and imagination. The right brain is also more capable of seeing the big picture. Its position on the right side of Etz Chaim, as the sefirah Chochmah, reminds us that Kaballah is mysticism and mysticism often and, with pleasure, defies traditional ideas about how to do things and how to think about things. While not prescriptive, mysticism is persuasive and rooted in the same traditions that reject it. Sufism is another example of how mysticism's soulful viewpoints threaten institutional forces in the religious traditions from which it springs.

But the wisdom of the Kabbalists is not limited to one hemisphere of the brain. Rich in intricacy, rooted in Tradition, and steeped in theological exploration, the intellectual rigor of the Kabbalists is not to be ignored, as the left side of the brain is actively working in concert with the right.

Many people can expand their capabilities to encompass both sides of the brain. However, the Kabbalists have synthesized their thinking to a remarkable degree, creating a voluminous library of theological and philosophical legacy which stands as a glorious example of wisdom.

The Kabbalists, dedicating their efforts with one goal in mind – tikkun – created their cosmology by applying the unified brain, just as the sefirot are "attached and unified" in the third "Holy" of Isaiah 6:3.

In this grand scheme of unification through agents like the sefirot and their scribes, the Kabbalists – grandsons of the King – present the unified, holistic thinking of the sages, including the authors of Sefer ha-Habir, as a materialization of God's Glory, via the Divinely created human mind. These are the heirs of glory, described in Proverbs 3: 35.

And in the world of Kabbalah, what is the ultimate manifestation of God's Glory?

It is the repair of Creation – the final healing of God's relationship with humanity, in tikkun, facilitated by wisdom.

10 Commandments and 613 Mitzvot

"Aaron lifted his hands toward the people and blessed them, and he came down after sacrificing the sin offering, the burnt offering, and the offering of wellbeing."

Leviticus 9: 22

At the beginning of Section IV, this verse is examined, with the question posed as to why Aaron raises his hands. The response points out that his two hands, like ours, have five fingers each, for a total of ten – equivalent in number to the sefirot.

And further, equivalent to the number of Commandments given to Moses. The text in Section IV explains that the number of letters in the 10 Commandments is 613, equivalent to the number of mitzvot. It states that all the Hebrew alphabet letters are also present in the Ten Commandments, except the letter Tet.

This is explained by Tet's identification with the human stomach, which has no equivalent in the sefirot. In this, the writers of Sefer ha-Bahir identify the Commandments given to Moses with the ten sefirot and with the human body.

The next question the text poses is why the sefirot were given this name. The explanation states that Psalm 19: 1 is the reason for that name, as it reads, "The heavens are telling the glory of God." The intimation is that the sefirot are doing the same.

The word for "telling" (or declare) is me-saprim in the text, most likely to serve the writer's purpose, which is to identify the sefirot as God's Glory in Creation. As emanations of the Divine, the "ten sefirot of nothingness" or the "10 ineffable sefirot", as described in Sefer Yetzirah, are not separate from God. They are how humans discern God in Creation.

In stanza 138, we again encounter raising hands to heaven with the 10 Commandments and the ten sefirot. In this instance, Moses raises his hands (Exodus 17: 11). The text explains that when he does so, "Israel prevails," with Israel described as an "Attribute" and further, "the Torah of Truth."

The Torah of Truth is explained in the text in relation to mystical – and physical – Israel as one of the "10 sayings" on which the world stands, with the ten fingers of two hands, uplifted to heaven, paralleling the ten sayings (remembering, of course, the ten utterances by which Creation was brought into being by the voice and will of God).

When Moses and Aaron (the first priest) raised their hands to heaven, they called on those ten utterances or sayings for the sake of Israel. For without victory for Israel over its enemies, the Torah of Truth (Israel) could not stand, and if Israel could not stand, Creation couldn't, either.

The Ten Sayings

In stanza 141, the question, "What are the ten sayings?" is posed, followed by a lengthy exposition on the utterances, aka the sefirot.

Let's journey through this Section of Sefer Ha-Bahir to discover a uniquely Mishnaic way of talking about the sefirot.

The first saying is corresponded to the Crown (Keter), with its people cast as Israel. Citing Psalm 100: 3, the writer of this stanza points to the spelling of the word "we" in verse, "Know that the LORD his God. It is he that made us, and we are his", with "we" being spelled lamed aleph. It's explained that lamed aleph could mean "to Aleph," meaning that the people are God's (with God cast as Aleph, the first letter of the Hebrew alphabet).

The second of the sayings is Wisdom (Chochmah), explained helped by Proverbs 8:22, "The LORD created me at the beginning of his work, the first of his acts of long ago." Next, it cites Psalm 111: 10, "The fear of the LORD is the beginning of wisdom."

Wisdom is cited as the first of God's acts, corresponding roughly to Adam Kadmon's model as the repository of God's Ideal Primordial Man. But in Psalm 111, it's a fear of the Divine that's located as the site from which wisdom grows.

This ties in with the idea of limiting the human capacity for wisdom. Knowing our limitations as creatures is key to healing the relationship with God. There's a strong element here of toeing the line drawn in the sands of the desert at Sinai - that we are to stop at understanding things that are "too difficult for us," leaving them to the ineffable mind of the concealed God to sort out.

Next, the text moves on to the third saying, which is unnamed as a sefirot but described as a "quarry." The text relates that from this quarry, "all the letters of Torah" were carved and that Torah is the rock on which the faithful stand - the Divine.

The fourth saying is chesed (lovingkindness), which is mentioned near the end of the stanza but is described as "the charity of God," with chesed characterized as "kindness."

Another unnamed sefirot/saying occurs in the instance of the 5th of these, in stanza 145, with the themes of fire and angels. This saying is explicitly described as "the great fire of the Blessed Holy One." One can assume this represents Hod (Glory) but lacks a positive identifier.

Still, the writer's reference to Deuteronomy 18:16 leaves little doubt: "This is what you requested of the LORD your God at Horeb on the day of the assembly when you said, 'If I hear the voice of the LORD my God any more, or ever again see this great fire, I will die.'"

This can only refer to the sefirah Hod. As we've said earlier in this book, it was the Mt. Horeb theophany which caused the people to "see" voices. Terrified, they huddled together, senses scrambled into a fine mush by God's confounding Glory, sending Moses into the Cloud alone.

Within this fearsome glory are the Chayot ha-Kadesh – the Angels, to the right and the Seraphim (Angels of fire) to the left. These are the highest of the high in the Hebrew angelic hierarchy, fully present to God's Glory. The text then gets to the point – the fear.

God's Glory is not a gentle thing. It is fiery, and it has enforcers devoted to praising the Divine and serving it. This is explained employing Ezekiel 1:18, "Their rims were tall and awesome, for the rims of all four were full of eyes all around."

God's Glory has eyes – lots and lots of eyes. This is a description of the Merkabah (Chariot) in which Elijah ascended to Heaven. A symbol of God's Glory, a reminder to readers of the awe-inspiring Chariot, is inserted into the text by way of illustration.

I'd imagine that if I were to see a wheel embedded with eyes that I would probably never sleep again. I would be afraid. I would begin wisdom because I would not want to know anything more about that chariot or to see it ever again, fearing I might die if I did. Just like the people at Mt. Horeb, I would gladly send Moses into that Cloud all alone, never to see whatever fearsome sight or hear whatever nerve-shredding sound the Almighty might be hiding in there. Chariot wheels embedded with eyes are just the tip of the iceberg with such a fearsome God!

At the sixth saying, things get murky again. Stanza 146 describes it as "the Throne of Glory, crowned, included, praised and hailed." It says that the sixth saying is Olam Haba/the World to Come, referencing wisdom as the saying's home.

The text then cites Genesis 1:3 and the creation of light, describing two different lights – one commanded and one created, distinguishing between the creative command and the finished product.

One of these two lights was stored away by the Creator "for the righteous in the World to Come," referencing Psalm 31.20, "In the shelter of your presence you hide them from human plots; you hold them safe under your shelter from contentious tongues." So, this primordial utterance commanding light was too much for humans to behold. From the mind of God, the thought of the light, borne into the nascent Creative Order on Divine Breath, is the pure form of the finished product. In direct contact with humanity, that light is unbearable, just as it was at Mt. Horeb. Fearsome and mindboggling, only the righteous will see it in Olam Haba.

Reading through the description of the sixth saying, we come to the 32 paths of wisdom. These are intimately related to the sefirot, as the 22 letters of the Hebrew alphabet and the ten utterances by which Creation came to be, as described in Sefer Yetzirah.

In Sefer ha-Bahir, the 32 paths of wisdom are described as the goodness of Creation, given as a gift to humanity, citing Proverbs 4: 2, "...for I give you good precepts, do not forsake my teaching". In other words, the raw material is there, but humanity must, to realize its Covenant with the Divine, dig for it. This is referred to in the text as Oral Torah, described as a "treasury" (perhaps the "quarry" mentioned above).

So, the Glory of God is fire and light, shared to the Created Order in a diluted form, while the undiluted form awaits the ascension of the righteous to the World to Come, as the 32 pathways lead us toward its Divine precincts, shovels in hand. Again, wisdom and glory are delineated and continually underlined in the Sefer ha-Bahir, making the conflation unavoidable.

Following a lengthy discussion of the necessity of suffering to the estate of righteousness, we come, finally to the seventh saying.

Again, there are no sefirot explicitly named, but the saying is described as first "Aravot" and then, as "Shamayim," both translated as "heaven" in the text. But in Hebrew, "Aravot" is a willow branch, associated with the Festival of Sukkot, celebrating God's protection in the Sinai desert (also called the Feast of Tabernacles or Booths), referencing the Wilderness Experience and Covenant, again.

Shamayim is part of the three-part cosmology of Judaism, identified as "heaven," with eretz as the earth and Sheol as the underworld.

The text then describes the seventh saying as the "same" as the sixth. In other words, the same as the glory/wisdom that is God's alone, eventually to be shared with the righteous alone, in Olam Haba. The text next relates that the seventh saying is both the same as the sixth and separate, as it relates to us that Holiness is among us. The seventh saying is then located by the text in the east as the seed of Israel, with Isaiah 43: 5 cited, as it reads, "I will bring your offspring from the east." The Cloud of Mt. Horeb, no longer visible, continues in its presence among the Israelites.

We finally arrive at the Eighth Saying in stanza 168. Again, there is no mention of a sefirot, but the text centers on the human body, and the Covenant of Circumcision is usually accomplished on a baby boy's 8th day of life.

There follows an explanation of the "8 directions in man", which are:

- "Right and left hands
- Right and left legs
- The head, the body, and the Covenant as arbiter
- And his wife, who is his mate."

In Sefer ha-Bahir's model, the Covenant mediates between the head and the body, creating a consubstantiality Sartre might have envied: a supernatural pineal gland of sorts. It further adds Primordial Eve in the form of the wife as part of man's body. This can be seen as a discouraging reminder of the position of women through most of history, but in terms of this book, it's supported exegetically with Genesis 2: 24, "Therefore, a man leaves his father and his mother and clings to his wife, and they become one flesh."

These eight parts of a man's body are then held up as paralleling the practice of circumcising baby boys on the 8th day, anthropomorphizing the Covenant, and co-opting the female sex, both now parts of man's body, to arrive at 8.

When we arrive at the 9th Saying, we discover that again, there is no corresponding sefirah and that it's combined, in the text, with the 10th. The effect is the feeling that someone was more interested in another aspect of the text, did not wish to hazard an embellishment of another writer's work, ran out of gas, or possibly that the text was somehow garbled or reconstructed over time.

But the Section continues (with possibly another writer taking the wheel) to expand on the two final sayings, referring to them as "two wheels." Netzach (Victory) then enters the discussion, with the "Victory of Victories described as "the end of the Divine Presence" in stanza 170. This points to Shekinah, the sefirah of Divine Presence, existing in the flesh of the earth, feeding Etz Chaim with its emanation of concealed Glory.

But what is meant by the Victory of Victories being "the end of the Divine Presence"? The Divine Presence, as an emanation of God, is not required in the World to Come as a sefirah or as a saying, for the need for emanations expires at its genesis.

The Divine Presence is now the fullness of that light we spoke of earlier, held apart through time for only the righteous to enjoy in Olam Haba.

Chapter Nine: Modern Scholarship and Kabbalah's Relationship to Physics

"The purpose of life is learning. The purpose of learning is to grasp the Divine."

Abraham Abulafia

As we've touched on in the last chapter, all we know about Kabbalah and its canon is handed down through generations of scribes and scholars. These are the minds that connected the disparate dots of the ages and gifted humanity with the rich legacies of Jewish Mysticism and Judaism itself.

But in the story of the Sefer ha-Bahir and public consciousness about it in modern times, two of these scholars stand out. These were Gershom Scholem, once one of the world's foremost authorities on Jewish Mysticism, and Aryeh Kaplan (1934 – 1983): author of Sefer ha-Bahir's translation we've used throughout this journey of discovery, encountering the major themes of this fascinating text.

If you're finding interest in this book, then I highly recommend the work of these modern scholars, both of whom contributed so lavishly to Sefer ha-Bahir's study and dissemination beyond its intended audience. Their contributions, I hope, will be of interest.

Gershom Scholem

While not all concur with Scholem's hypotheses or methodology, no one can say that he is not a giant of Jewish religious scholarship, especially in the realm of Kabbalah. His Major Trends in Jewish Mysticism (1941) has enjoyed three printings and was re-published in 2011. To this day, the work stands as a comprehensive, unchallenged masterpiece of Kabbalah scholarship, tracing its roots from antiquity through 18th Century Ashkenazi Hassidism.

Gershom Scholem was a prolific writer about Kabbalah, penning 40 books and 700 articles in his lifetime. Martin Buber once described him as one who had "created a whole academic discipline" – namely, the study of Kabbalah, for motivations other than Faith.

Scholem's interest in the Sefer ha-Bahir was first signaled by his doctoral thesis about the book in 1922. In 1923, his father's publishing house released the young Scholem's book on the subject. In his doctoral studies, Scholem decided that his life's work would be the Kabbalah. He believed that Kabbalah could spark a major revival in Judaism due to its intricate expositions about humanity's relationship with God, especially Jewish humanity.

Scholem's German-language exploration of the Bahir came with copious footnotes, referencing Kabbalistic masters who'd quoted the text. Clearly, Scholem had read and absorbed much of the Kabbalistic literature available to him.

In 1928, Scholem authored an article expanding on his earlier work, linking Provence and Spain to developing the mystical movement, which had its apex in the Zohar. Then, in 1948, he published The Beginning of the Kabbalah. He continued to expand

and correct this book over many years, never satisfied with his work's integrity.

Scholem saw Kabbalah as arising from religion (its history and study) rather than as a work of pure philosophy, despite his secular orientation. As we noted in the book in this series addressing Sefer Yetzirah, it's indisputable that Kabbalistic history movements have drawn their spiritual parallels from Jewish history, regardless of the content that might be seen as philosophical influences or incursions. Of particular interest is Scholem's hypothesis that the Lurianic model of Creation – an apocalyptic shattering - was a response to the Spanish Expulsion of 1492. The impact of Jewish history on Kabbalah, Scholem rightly pointed out, influenced its development, giving birth to concepts like Shevirot ha Kelim. As the Jewish presence in Spain was shattered, so was the universe at Creation.

Scholem's contention concerning Luria's Creation model led the scholar to coin the term "historiosophy": the conjunction of metaphysics with history. The idea has penetrated scholarly circles in many disciplines, including the study of the European Holocaust. Applying a philosophy of history through a metaphysical lens is a tremendous contribution to numerous fields of scholarship.

With this approach came the contention that Sefer ha-Bahir was a link, joining together Early Jewish Mysticism and the later doctrine of emanations of the Divine in the form of the sefirot. Part of Scholem's hypothesis is concerned with the Gnostics – a sect existing in the Ancient Near East, not only in Judaism but in the Pagan and Christian religions starting in the 1st Century, as evidenced in related writings.

Acknowledging Sefer ha-Bahir's Ancient origins, possibly rooted in Raza Rabba, Scholem posited a Gnostic element in the book's genesis while acknowledging that the bulk of Sefer ha-Bahir's development occurred in the Middle Ages, in various contexts.

And it's clear that Scholem was correct in his assessment of Kabbalah as an enlivening agent for a renewed Jewish spirituality. However, I'm not sure he'd be pleased to see Kabbalah Centers springing up from LA to Warsaw, for that is not the Kabbalah of the sages and scholars. But Kabbalah has penetrated Judaism at heart in recent decades, enriching the practice of millions of Jews.

Lately, the Kabbalah's influence, especially among the younger generations, has led to developing yet another discipline of academic study, growing from the one established by Scholem – the modernization of Kabbalah. This development suggests that Kabbalah has already taken root outside its usual home – that of the Hassidim. As Gershom Scholem suggested, Kabbalah has set a fire of renewed spirituality among modern Jews.

The Kabbalah of Gershom Scholem is the source of something. He knew that. While not a traditional Jew in the Orthodox sense, it's clear that Scholem's interest in Kabbalah was not purely academic. In Kabbalah, he saw a flame that could catch fire, providing modern Jews with a connection to their history that was profound, spiritual, and almost enfleshed, in its presence among them and kinship with them.

Aryeh Kaplan

As I've made readers aware, this volume draws on Aryeh Kaplan's translation of Sefer ha-Bahir. A master of both physics and Kabbalah, Aryeh Kaplan is also remembered as one of the driving forces behind the baal teshuvah movement through his written work, which means "master of repentance," in the late 1950s/1960s movement called Jews to Traditional Jewish Orthodoxy.

Rather the antithesis of Gershom Scholem, Aryeh Kaplan was an Orthodox rabbi. But like Scholem, he was a prolific author, calling Jews to his version of holiness. Kaplan also wrote three books about Jewish meditation, as a proponent and practitioner, among an impressive canon of works numbering over 50 books, addressing

Hebrew Scripture, Jewish Mysticism, and Jewish liturgical subjects and translations.

One of his most popular books, even today, is the one he wrote about Sefer ha-Bahir (1957). Another is his book about the Sefer Yetzirah (1997). Much like Gershom Scholem, his scholarship on Sefer ha-Bahir is famed for its contribution to the study of the book. He was instrumental in greatly increasing interest in both Bahir and Yetzirah and contributed to the enlivening presence of Kabbalah in our contemporary world, even beyond Judaism.

An ardent teacher, his ability to clarify and illuminate texts is apparent in the translation of Sefer ha-Bahir we've been using in this book. Aryah Kaplan made a book that mystified those who encountered it for centuries accessible to English speakers. And while Sefer ha-Bahir is esoteric literature in every possible sense, Kaplan's work has helped to make sense of it, as Scholem's has.

Perhaps there was a common purpose between the two, in some mysterious way. With Scholem suggesting and advancing that Kabbalah might enliven modern Judaism and Kaplan calling Jews to Orthodoxy, the methodologies and desired outcomes diverged, but the spirit in which each Kabbalah Master approached his life's work seems the same. For both, Kabbalah was a consuming passion, as it has been for a long line of scribes and scholars in the great tradition of Jewish Mysticism. While these two Kabbalah Masters belong to the mid-20th Century, an eruption of such ardor in the Modern Era is significant. The 20th Century's extreme rationalism and insistence on empiricism also made it the Century of Genocide for Jews, manifesting in the apocalyptic horror of the Holocaust. In the ardor of Scholem and Kaplan is a desire to find a coherent response to tortured rationalizations for genocide and humanity that had descended into the abyss.

Kabbalah and its Masters found a balance between the two hemispheres of the brain, providing a full-throated response to the

Modern Era's rationalism. With Kabbalah and its mystical approach to Creation and humanity's role in it, it's arguable this elusive balance finds a home in Kabbalah. While there's little to suggest this philosophical equilibrium has influenced world events, it might be said, in Kabbalistic terms, that tikkun has a friend in the growing influence of Kabbalah.

Aryeh Kaplan started his life as a physicist, leaving that calling for another - to be a traditional Orthodox rabbi. Just as Scholem consciously decided that Kabbalah would be his life's work, Kaplan chose the passion of Kabbalah. While the two lived out their devotion to the idea of a Jewish Renaissance driven by Kabbalistic principles in markedly different ways, the results moved Jewish Mysticism forward with decidedly different motivations. And in moving it forward, it seems that another Kabbalistic subgroup of academic study has been founded.

Kaplan's early life as a physicist is of great interest in any Jewish Mysticism discussion due to his modern role in enlarging its canon and influence. In recent times, Kabbalah's presence has been felt in the realm of science, with parallels being drawn between its descriptions of Creation and Physics. This development has generated even more interest in books like Sefer ha-Bahir and may hold the key to re-aligning humanity's thinking as we move forward in the 21st Century.

The Kabbalah of Physics

Whether you're interested in Physics or not, Physics is interested in you, as its purpose is to study and understand nature. More precisely, Physics' mission is to interpret the properties and behaviors of matter as it moves through time and space in its exchanges with energy.

Is this not reminiscent of the Kabbalistic exploration of time and space, with the discussion of "created light" versus "light in the process of being created"? Whether you think so or not, science has latched onto what is increasingly being perceived as a parallel between the two realms in terms of the interplay between matter and energy.

In both systems of thought and interpretation, energy and matter are unified - part of the same complex. They are not, as has been advanced in the distant past, separate realities that may be transformed one into the other but are both parts of a unified and inviolable whole.

The radical dualism between the two was the problem Descartes (1596 - 1650) was attempting to rectify in his Letter to the Learned Doctors of the Sorbonne. In Descartes' case, the matter in question was that of the body in relation to the "mind/soul," attempting to reconcile matter with energy while claiming a distinct ontology for both. The work of Renee Descartes, in this regard, is universally recognized as having moved the question of material's consubstantiality with the spiritual/emotional forward, despite the dualistic premise advanced. But in stating that, "To perceive a mode (mind/soul) apart from its substance requires an intellectual abstraction." Descartes exposes the problem with dualism as advanced in his work.

But the science of the 21st Century understands the universe as a unity. This is also the Kabbalistic conception of matter and spirit/mind - as an inviolable unity. Moving parts are integral to the whole, and in this model, the mind/soul is one with the body, just as the concealed God is one with Creation. While unseen and immaterial, God creates and interacts with matter by various means - speech, light, theophany, dreams, and visions. The human mind is rooted in the same Divine/scientific template.

As Einstein explained in his Special Theory of Relativity, matter, and energy are exchangeable, one with the other. In complete unity, they share a source. They are the same, exchanging properties and behaviors as required by existing conditions. This reality precludes the need for "transformation."

Quantum Electrodynamics has reconciled the Theory of Special Relativity with Quantum Physics, contending that the entire universe is in the process of continual evolution. In this model, energy and matter are destroyed spontaneously with their creation.

Does any of this remind readers of the Breaking of the Vessels (Shevirot ha kelim)?

The matter-energy duality of Einstein's Theory is the central tenet of Jewish Mysticism – that all that exists, whether material or energetic/spiritual/intellectual, is part of a whole and indivisible from its source and ontology. While free to exchange and interact, the material and the energetic are manifestations of the same overarching reality – this is the precise contention at the heart of Kabbalah – that all is Divinely inspired and created, thus unified and manifesting diversely. What may appear to be separate and yet, exists as an aspect or feature of the whole might as well be called an emanation. The sefirot, for example, exist independently and yet operates collaboratively. As emanations of the Divine, there is no separation between their Divine source and them, as the sefirot emanate the Divine properties and attributes into Creation.

While concealed, the Divine is ever emanating into Creation the light of Ohr Ein Sof hiding in plain sight as "created light." Cloaked and limited, the Light of the Limitless comes to us as part of our material world while yet Divine. Matter and energy united in perfect purpose.

There is no "observer" and "observed" in the Quantum Physics/Kabbalistic viewpoint. In observing, the observer has a material impact on the observed, as the observation's energetic influence is material. Energy and material being of the same stuff, there is no identification of one or the other without a challenge to the system's unity.

That humanity's actions have both a material and "immaterial" impact on the world around it is analogous to the idea of tikkun as the response to the brokenness of Creation. While all exist in integrity, it's clear that this principle, in both Physics and Kabbalah, bears out in the real world. The most obvious example is the effect on the physical environment of our actions (androgenic climate change, extinction events, catastrophic weather events). These actions have a physical basis, but they're rooted in a spiritual or philosophical vacuum. This vacuum typifies the Modern Era, which remains adhered to Descartes and an earlier understanding of matter and energy as two separate things. Just as matter and energy are not two separate things, humanity and Creation are not.

And there is a commensurate impact on the human spirit/intellect. As the world reacts to humanity's poor stewardship, humanity either doubles down and becomes even more abusive or falls into a depressive state. In either instance, the spiritual and intellectual faculties are compromised. On the one hand, that aware person sees Creation under stress and knows that she's at least partially responsible. Real-world indicators of humanity's impending extinction (COVID-19 and other pandemic events in the 21st Century) are depressing, triggering existential anxiety. But the cognitive dissonance inherent in acknowledging climate change and the demand it makes for humanity to change is met with a wall of denial to prevent it from infiltrating the minds of those too fragile to accommodate it.

Jewish Mysticism calls the practitioner to action. Built into the model is humanity's role as both partners in Creation and key to its healing. Whether the action is rooted in prayer and the satisfaction of the mitzvot or the popular conception of tikkun as the healing of injustice through righteous acts, actions have a decisive impact on the material and spiritual world. The healing of one is the healing of the other. The healing of Creation is the healing of humanity.

Because, while independent, they are made of the same stuff. The breath that enlivened the mud doll is that of the Creator, divinely animating humans with the very exhalations of the concealed, creating God. Even the mud from which that humble doll was once formed by the hand of the Creator signals sacredness: formed of the dirt of the earth, recently created by the same imaginative force.

In this emerging discipline of the Kabbalah as a parallel to Physics, new scholarship is continually being produced. One such notable scholar in this nascent tradition is Eduard Shyfrin.

The author of the book, *From Infinity to Man*, Shyfrin joins an innumerable procession of sages, scholars, academics, and Holy Men. Once a Soviet metallurgist, Shyfrin is today an observant Jew and a follower of Kabbalah, making teshuvah (a return to Jewish Orthodoxy) and discovering a renewed and vibrant Jewish faith, illuminated by Kabbalah's mysticism.

Like the academic intellectual turned Kabbalah Master, Gershom Scholem and the physicist turn rabbi and Kabbalah Master, Aryeh Kaplan, Shyfrin bring together worlds unaccustomed to collaboration, uniting and illuminating them for humanity hungry for revelation.

Chapter Ten: The End of Neo-Platonism and the Divine Presence

"The word beginning (Reshit) is nothing other than wisdom."

Sefer ha-Habir, Section I, stanza 3

The Sefer ha-Bahir has been one of the most influential works in the development of Kabbalah over many centuries. With the Sefer Yetzirah and the Zohar, the Bahir stands as a cornerstone in the canon of Kabbalistic writings.

Any Kabbalistic work of any import contains at least one quotation from its pages. Nachmanides cited it as an authoritative source in his Torah commentary. Through time, this fragmentary book, passing through the hands of multiple scribes, is one of the most influential and foundational works of Kabbalah. It was Gershom Scholem himself who identified Sefer ha-Bahir as the first of all Kabbalistic works to present the symbolism of later Kabbalah.

In its descriptions of the sefirot alone, Sefer ha-Bahir provides a central theme for later Kabbalistic sages, including Luria himself. Influenced by the contemporary misfortunes of Jews in distant Spain from his home in Safed, Israel, Luria drew on the Spanish Expulsion, finding in it a unifying moment to illustrate the hope implicit in the Shevirot ha Kelim – eventual healing in tikkun.

But the sefirot of Sefer ha-Bahir are not the sefirot of Yetzirah and later Kabbalah. In this book, they're not described as emanations. They're described as powers or as hypostasis - the immutable, underlying reality of all things. In this instance, that reality is the Divine. It's in Sefer Yetzirah that we see the characterization of the sefirot as emanations, although both works share the idea of the 32 paths of wisdom, more fulsomely delineated in Yetzirah.

Because we've just talked about Physics and the Kabbalah, now is an opportune time to turn to the Hellenistic ideas expressed in the text of Sefer ha-Bahir. In the Ancient Near East, cross-pollination of religious and philosophical ideas was inevitable. In this cauldron of competing for cultural/spiritual identities and belief systems (because spiritual systems and culture were synonymous in these societies) and intellectual ideas, there was no chance of ideas being untainted by those of one's neighbors.

But is it a "taint" or stain, or is it a normal interchange of ideas that find common ground between them? One religion's "syncretism" (the incursion of one religion's claims into another) is another religion's growth.

For this purpose, I'd like to present the work of Abraham bar Hiyya la-Nasi (1070 to c. 1136). This Medieval Barcelona Kabbalist was also a philosopher, astrologer, and mathematician. He's believed to be the person responsible for transmitting the Arabic system of algebra to the Christians of Europe. His best-known book, Hibbur ha Meshihah ve-ha-Tishboret, about algebra, and practical geometry, containing the first known example of the quadratic equation.

It's helpful to understand that Tishboret influenced Leonardo Fibonacci's thinking as you read more about this Spanish Kabbalist, one of the most influential of his time and in the matter of Sefer ha-Bahir, a contributing author.

Before exploring bar Hiyya's work in the Sefer ha-Bahir, we'll turn toward the Greeks to refresh our understanding of the Neo-Platonic idea of "forms" and how they influenced the sage's thinking.

Forms vs. Matter

Neo-Platonism was a Platonic revival that prompted a school of thought. It was more a popular way of thinking than a system of thought or philosophical school. While it's tracked to the 5th century CE in terms of documents, its influence has been tremendous on Judaism, Christianity, and Islam. If you scratch these Three Monotheistics in the right place, you'll find a distinct scent of Neo-Platonism.

Derived from Plato and Aristotle (who disagreed on the theory of forms in key aspects), the theory of forms casts the material as mutable (subject to change) and ideas (forms) as immutable (not subject to change). This means that ideas are the substance and unchangeable reality of all we know. And all we know in the material world is just a reasonable facsimile of its true and incorruptible form.

The bubbling stewpot of Ancient Near Eastern ideas was the ideal birthplace for an intellectual process to be applied to thinking about the big questions. Neo-Platonism, a catchall of a range of religious and cultural ideas, reflects the region's cross-cultural vitality in that time.

Philo was a Jewish Hellenist who saw Judaism through the lens of Plato, Stoicism, and other Greek influences. Philo believed that only an ecstatic experience could reveal God's true nature to the believer, while Christians like Justin Martyr sought to forward a synthesis of Platonism with Christianity.

In Plato, there is also a rejection of matter in favor of ideas/forms. This is expressed in Early Christianity in figures like Origen (who castrated himself to be less subject to his body's urges) and Augustine, who wished, in his Confessions, that he could eat food as he would medicine – taking it only when necessary. Food interrupted the more important matters at hand – those of the spirit and forms.

Abraham bar Hiyya and Sefer ha-Bahir

Gershom Scholem first noticed distinct similarities between the approach in bar Hiyya's Hegyon ha-Nefesh (Contemplation of the Soul) and the description of the creation process in Section I of Sefer ha-Bahir. The common denominator, of course, is far beyond writing style. What was prominent in Scholem's discovery was the Neo-Platonist thought evident in both texts.

Pivotal is "tohu wa bohu" (Formless and void). In Sefer ha-Bahir and bar Hiyya's Tishboret, from the formless and void matter and form both come to be. Lifeless and amorphous, tohu wa bohu is animated by the hand of the Divine. In this action, according to a Neo-Platonist reading of the text, form and matter are combined as necessary facilitation of Creation.

In stanza 11 of Section I of Sefer ha-Bahir, we read, "He created Desolation (Bohu) and placed it in Peace, and He created Chaos (Tohu) and placed it in Evil."

Here, we see that the formless and void splits into matter and form, with Bohu adopting form (the Divine element of Creation) and Tohu adopting matter (chaos).

This is also an attempt to reconcile items in the Hebrew Scriptures like Isaiah 45: 7, which reads, "I form light and create darkness, I make weal and create woe; I the LORD do all these things." By explaining their dual presence as a cosmic synergetic event, forms and matter unite, redeeming matter. But there is a further explanation of this event in stanza 14.

Light is used as an example of something which exists because it was created. But of darkness, Sefer ha-Bahir says, "...there was no making, only separation and set aside."

This refers to Genesis 1:4b, which reads, "And God separated the light from the darkness." What's being implied is that darkness is like a divider in a three-ring binder. It separates things. It doesn't have the same meaning as the rest of the created order.

The sense is that Neo-Platonic thinking not only somewhat demonizes matter but fails to give God the benefit of the doubt with the presence of evil in Creation. This element of the discussion of matter and form undermines later Kabbalah, which defines the presence of evil almost as a means for humanity to redeem itself. It also ignores that a God who creates evil and good is unquestionably omnipotent and ineffable, beyond feeble human reasoning.

Just as there is no perception of light without a perception of darkness, there is no perception of evil without good. As we discussed briefly in the second chapter of this book, the theme of tension is a recurring one in Kabbalah and most discussion of monotheistic religions. That tension – between good and evil - provides humanity with choices or free will. The same tension presents us with a God who is both immanent and transcendent, simultaneously.

What's been developed from this Neo-Platonist means of describing the Creation event is a process of the Neo-Platonist thinking present in Sefer ha-Bahir and other Medieval Kabbalistic works being subsumed under the mother Tradition itself. Luria's conception of the Shevirot ha-Kelim is a vision of Creation rooted in both Scriptural Tradition and contemporary and Ancient Jewish history. In every shattering of the Jewish people, there is Luria's grand model and plan for redemption and healing.

And this model and plan meshes with modern Physics so tidily. As Kabbalistic thinking has developed, the Hellenistic whispers in its pages stand in witness to an age of intellectual growth that moved from the Ancient Near East to Europe and beyond. And as Kabbalah has gained influence, it comes to the wider world as its own highly developed system of internal criticism and questioning.

The story of Abraham bar Hiyya is yet another way the Sefer ha-Bahir tells us a long and fascinating story of intellectual and religious currents interacting and fusing as part of an epic journey of becoming something.

Next, we need to discuss a key distinguishing feature of the Sefer ha-Bahir that we can't leave our exploration of the text without talking about – the role of Shekhinah. That role is that of the Divine Presence in Creation.

Shekhinah, Divine Presence

Only mentioned in Bahir by name once in Section V, stanza 75, the idea of Shekhinah is discussed in the text as the Divine Presence and associated with wisdom and tzedakah (righteousness). Again, wisdom is associated with glory, represented by the indwelling Presence of the Divine.

We encounter Shekhinah in Bahir as follows: "The first 'righteousness' is literal righteousness (Tzedek). This is the Divine Presence (i.e., Shekinah). It is thus written (Isaiah 1:21), "Righteousness dwells in it."

But before we can penetrate the verse and its place in the Bahir, let's find out a little more about whom we're discussing.

The word is taken from the Hebrew root meaning "dwell, settle or inhabit." Implied is the idea of a place for God and God's creatures to live. With Shekinah, the word refers to God, specifically. Shekinah is also interpreted as the Holy Spirit of God in Judaism (Ruach hakodesh). The word is also interpreted to mean a "manifestation of God's glory."

The name first appears in the Targum (the Aramaic language version of the Hebrew Scriptures), which began to be transcribed in the middle of the 1st Century CE as "Shakinta." The name Shekhinah also appears in the Talmudic and Midrashic sources.

Regarding the sefirot, Shekhinah is associated with the sefirah, Malchut, which is set at the base of Etz Chaim. The indwelling Shekhinah/Divine Presence is represented, like Malchut/Kingdom, as being both parts of and set apart from the Tree of Life.

As associated with Malchut, Shekhinah is the temporary manifestation of God's glory, as the concealed God awaits our efforts toward tikkun. This stopgap glory is a glimpse of the Divine and a preview of the main attraction. Both emanative sefirah and the manifestation of the Divine in Creation, Shekhinah is more than a ray of created light. Shekhinah is much more like the scent of a good perfume being detected with delight long after the wearer has left the room.

Returning to our stanza from Sefer ha-Bahir, we encounter Shekhinah as "literal righteousness" or the "first righteousness." When we come across the Divine Presence next in the text, in stanza 169, we read, "The end of the Divine Presence of the Blessed Holy One is under His feet. Thus, it is written (Isaiah 66:1), "The heaven is My throne, and the earth is the hassock for My feet."

Malchut/Shekhinah is in the earth that the Etz Chaim is planted in. The glory and presence of God nurture the Tree of Life from the earth's very core. God's Kingdom is "the hassock" for the feet of a transcendent God, immanent via emanation and the power of a holistic, unified Deity.

Shekhinah, the Universal Mother

The Kabbalistic story of Shekhinah tells the tale of a universal mother, sent on a mission to gather the sparks - the stray nitzotzot - that showered Creation at the Breaking of the Vessels. Like a mother hen, Shekhinah comes to pick the light out of the cracks in Creation so we can start putting it all back together again.

Shekhinah is the hope of repair in the Divine Presence, only here until we can get our act together. As Shekhinah partners with we poor slobs in this grand design into which a monkey wrench was thrown, the universal mother gathers lost sparks, enlivening Creation to generate its intended potential.

Much is made of the feminization of Shekhinah, as though God had biological sex. This anthropomorphization has led to many theological and exegetical explorations in search of the meaning of a "feminized" God. In the matter of adhering biological sex to God, I submit Isaiah 55:8-9, which reads, "For my thoughts are not your thoughts, nor are your ways my ways, says the LORD. For as the heavens are higher than the earth, so are my ways higher than your ways and my thoughts than your thoughts."

In other words, God is completely "other." The Divine may not be described - or named in the same way that the created are described and named. If God is unknowable and beyond our complete and confident understanding, then how does applying a creaturely, biological sex class to God even enter the discussion?

And so, Shekhinah may be depicted as a universal mother. Shekhinah may also be depicted as a mechanic with bulging muscles and a mustache. Shekhinah maybe a border collie, sniffing after lost sparks. But Shekhinah is not a square peg, a round hole, or a side of fries. Shekhinah is whatever Shekhinah will be, and so, for this book, I will studiously ignore all appeals to a sexed God, regardless of God's assignment as male, throughout recorded history.

If God is beyond the restrictions of the human intellect and of being named, as we've discovered it is the case, then God is also beyond the limitations of the human body.

Shekhinah may be characterized as both mother and father and neither. God being completely "other" precludes the anthropomorphization of whatever God was, is, or will be.

But Shekhinah is crucial to the story being told in the Bahir. The Divine Presence in the Created Order mentioned so peripherally in the text is more pivotal to the narrative of Creation's healing than any sexed label could ever illuminate.

So, let's return to the text of Sefer ha-Bahir to discover more.

The Victory of Victories

In stanza 170, we again find a reference to Neo-Platonist forms in the "7 Holy Forms". To explain the Divine Presence, the writer of this stanza refers again to the human body and its seven parts (with the 8th being the wife) as representing these "Holy Forms" (as discussed in Chapter 8 of this book). The Covenant of Circumcision, as you'll recall, mediates in the human body between the head and the rest of the body. In the 248 "positive" commandments, we also find the organs and bones of the human body, as described in stanza 168.

At the end of stanza 169, the text refers to the "victory of victories" or netzach netzachim, in Hebrew. The sefirah, Netzach/Victory, at the base of the column on the right-hand side of Etz Chaim, holds the key to understanding the import of this stanza and its relationship to the Divine Presence/Shekhinah.

Netzach may also be translated as "eternity" or "perpetuity." So, what the writer is talking about is something very decisive and final. The word also translates as "strength" or endurance, as found in the Hebrew Scriptures, from the word root nun tsady het. This adds an element of tension to the narrative, as the end of the Divine Presence is what's being discussed.

At the conclusion of stanza 171, we find the "Holy, Holy, Holy" of Isaiah 6:3, which ends with the phrase, "the whole earth is full of his glory."

The text describes a three-fold Presence, following Isaiah's words, saying that "victory is one" and "victories is two," for a total of three. But the point is that the Divine Presence exists in the Divine realms as much as it does in the Created Order. God is omnipresent, omniscient and omnipotent, and undivided. There is no difference, ontologically, between the Divine Presence and the Divine. They are the same, located variously.

The Divine Presence is again equated to wisdom in stanza 171, as "light that was derived from the first light, which is wisdom" and that "it also surrounds all things," using the Isaiah portion as evidentiary, scriptural support.

The text then expounds on the nature of the seven Holy Forms, describing a King and his seven sons, whom he instructs to sit one above the other. The son asked to sit at the bottom, furthest from the King, complains that he would prefer to be near his father. But the King says, "I will surround you and see you all day." This passage equates the King to God and the 8 "parts" of the human body, as discussed in chapter 8 and in the Divine Presence.

The Divine Presence is described in this stanza as a direct analog of God, available to the Created Order and "surrounding all things," making it possible for Creation to be full of God's glory.

The key to Shekhinah and the "victory of victories" is found near the end of stanza 169, in words "The end of the Divine Presence of the Blessed Holy One is under His feet, referencing Isaiah 66: 1, as discussed earlier in this chapter.

Creation becomes at footstool for the Divine, once again at home in the Creation wrought by the ten utterances. The Divine Presence "under His feet," ending the necessity for the Divine Presence in creation, as Daddy has come home.

The victory of victories in the final and holistic healing of Creation, with God's Presence, made total and visible through the realization of tikkun.

The wisdom of "first, literal righteousness," which is the sole province of the Divine, has made itself at home in Creation, putting up its feet, reconciled to itself in the fullness of a Divine Creator whose vision for this masterpiece has finally materialized.

But What About Netzach?

As the sefirah of victory, Netzach stands at the bottom of the "pillar of mercy," as the right-hand side of the Tree of Life is sometimes called.

What's special about that position?

This position in Etz Chaim places Netzach in the role of "facilitator." Netzach is there to do something important on behalf of the Divine. At the top of the Tree, including on the right side, are specific attributes of God's Divine Will. In these attributes are God's desires for the human creature.

As I've pointed out above, the meaning of the word "netzach" extends to "strength." It might also be interpreted as "patience." Paying attention to these interpretations renders Netzach a helper that provides humanity with its own will – to endure and persevere until the "victory of victories" is realized. Opposite Hod/Glory on the Tree, Netzach portrays the right leg/foot, while Hod portrays the left lower extremities.

Encompassing righteousness as a feature of God's glory, Hod works with Netzach to achieve the victory all Creation groans toward, the two sefirah moving the whole project forward.

The "victory of victories" (netzach netzachim) refers to the endurance/perseverance required to reach the reality of eternity – another definition of this Hebrew word. How do you define endurance or perseverance?

If you're running in a foot race, endurance refers to your ability to finish the race and to maintain performance throughout. In this instance, the race is tikkun, and the prize is eternity – an eternity lived out in the Divine Presence truly and fulsomely present in Creation. The realization of tikkun, in the satisfaction of God's Covenantal relationship with humanity via Mystical Israel, is held in the satisfaction of the contents of the Covenant – the ten commandments and the 613 mitzvot.

Netzach, in the world of Kabbalah, represents the endurance required to work toward a distant goal. It shines in the distance, urging us forward. And Shekhinah's departure from Creation does not mean that God has left us. It means that the concealed God is at last revealed, feet up and satisfied with the (finally) completed work.

Throughout Sefer ha-Bahir, the Divine Presence, while scantly present explicitly, is ever-present in the text. Described as the "first, literal righteousness" and as the ground from which wisdom springs. This is God's "stunt double" indwelling the Created Order as the source of the Divine's dreams for us. Here to witness to the Glory of God (in wisdom and righteousness), Shekhinah stands as the benchmark sefirah. For when Shekhinah leaves, the Divine arrives.

In the satisfaction of tikkun - the healing of the relationship between God and humanity - the Divine Presence withdraws, as it is no longer required in that role. With Creation Ordered as it was always intended to be, there is no more need for the stunt double. The protagonist has walked on the set and the director, at that moment, calls out, "that's a wrap."

Standing as a symbol of Mystical Israel, Shekhinah encompasses all God's dreams for humanity, related to the healing of a relationship blown out of the water with just one bite from an apple. Shattering vessels are recovered and repaired, and the Divine comes home, settling into the throne of the Created Order, feet comfortably set on the footstool of the earth.

As the credits roll, all is good in the newly revealed Light of the Limitless - finally returned from a long and painful exile, Olam Haba having been brilliantly achieved.

Conclusion

As you have seen, Sefer ha-Bahir is a wonder of ancient influence, Medieval scholarship, and modern interpretation, its strangeness less inaccessible than once believed. For that, we can be grateful to the work of countless Jewish scholars, scribes, and Kabbalah Masters, Gershom Scholem, and Aryeh Kaplan among them.

I hope this exploration of the Sefer ha-Bahir has increased your understanding of both the book and the long path of development taken by Kabbalah and Jewish Mysticism over the thousands of years the Jewish religion has existed.

Jewish Mysticism and the literature it has gifted the world with over centuries is undoubtedly one of the original mystical movements. Unquestionably, its presence may be read in the Hebrew Scriptures, where bones dance and people see voices and hear visions from a mountain on fire with the presence of God. But I know that mysticism is an organic phenomenon, emanating from the human spirit in communion with the great "I AM" (WAS, WILL BE).

And in that sense, the Sefer ha-Bahir reflects a vibrant, mystical tradition in Judaism, resulting not just from the contemplation of the Hebrew Scripture and accompanying literature but from the proximity to philosophical movements in the Ancient Near East. The influence of these movements continues in the Great Three Monotheists in numerous ways, with Sefer ha-Bahir being only one example. And the example demonstrates how that effect is possible, with the ideas in the book linking the ancient to the Medieval worlds.

For that reason, the document discussed in this book has tremendous value. Sefer ha-Bahir is both a spiritual treatise, fractured by time but representing a genesis of systematic thinking and as an example of the power of ideas to transform as time and cultures pass away. It's in that transformation that the very spirit of wisdom is found. Wisdom is transformative, evolving intelligence, lives, society, and history. Wisdom is a glory that reflects the Light of the Limitless. Wisdom can be as collective as it is individual.

In the Bahir, we discover both manifestations of wisdom, the synthesis of creaturely nature with Divine breath – matter and energy, exchanging and creating. Over time, the text's collective creation only highlights the individual contributions in its esoteric parables and shifting viewpoints, all straining toward that one conclusion – that all are redeemable.

I have been honored to share the story of Sefer ha-Bahir with you and hope it has increased your interest in the world of Jewish Mysticism and Kabbalah.

With that thought, I offer the Aaronic Blessing, as we part.

"The LORD bless you and keep you; the LORD make his face to shine upon you, and be gracious to you; the LORD lift up his countenance upon you, and give you peace."

Here's another book by Mari Silva that you might like

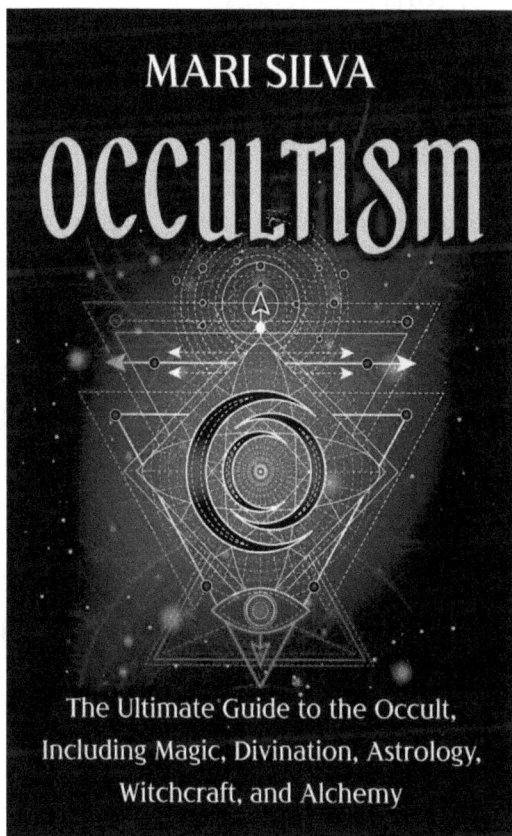

MARI SILVA

OCCULTISM

The Ultimate Guide to the Occult, Including Magic, Divination, Astrology, Witchcraft, and Alchemy

Your Free Gift (only available for a limited time)

Thanks for getting this book! If you want to learn more about various spirituality topics, then join Mari Silva's community and get a free guided meditation MP3 for awakening your third eye. This guided meditation mp3 is designed to open and strengthen ones third eye so you can experience a higher state of consciousness. Simply visit the link below the image to get started.

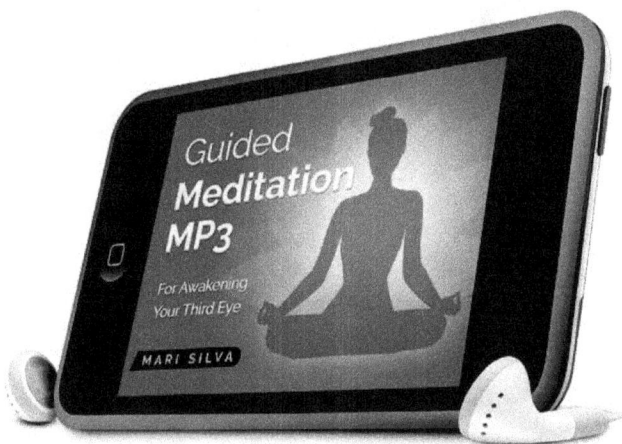

https://spiritualityspot.com/meditation

References

Arnoff, S.H., (n.d), The Concealed Face of God, New York, NY.

Ben, E., & Halevi, S. (1994). *ADAM AND THE KABBALISTIC TREE* Red Wheel Weiser

Dan, J. (1987). *THE ENIGMATIC BOOK BAHIR.* JSTOR Gershom Scholem and the Mystical Dimension of Jewish History, New York University Press https://www.jstor.org/stable/j.ctt9qg6m5.7?seq=1#metadata_info_tab_contents

Dubov, N.D., (n.d), Kelipot and Sitra Achra, Brooklyn

Hoffman, E., (n.d), *The Hebrew Alphabet: A Mystical Journey.* (n.d.). My Jewish Learning

https://www.myjewishlearning.com/article/the-hebrew-alphabet-a-mystical-journey/

Kaplan, A., 2001, The Bahir Illumination, Newburyport, MA, Red Wheel Weiser

Metzger, B.M., Murphy, R.E., 1991, The New Oxford Annotated Bible, New Revised Standard Version, New York, NY, Oxford University Press

www.ingramcontent.com/pod-product-compliance
Lightning Source LLC
Chambersburg PA
CBHW071902090426
42811CB00004B/711